REDISCOVERING
CATHOLICISM

REDISCOVERING
CATHOLICISM

JOURNEYING TOWARD OUR SPIRITUAL NORTH STAR

MATTHEW KELLY

Beacon
PUBLISHING

REDISCOVERING CATHOLICISM:
Journeying Toward Our Spiritual North Star.

First Edition published in 2002.
"Imagine this…" is a variation of a parable
by an anonymous author from an unknown source.

Library of Congress Cataloging-in Publication Data.

Kelly, Matthew
        Rediscovering Catholicism : journeying toward our spiritual
north star / Matthew Kelly, - first edition
        ISBN 1-929266-08-1 (cloth.)
1.Religion.   2. Catholicism   3. Spirituality
4. Kelly, Matthew.
I Title.

08 09 10 • 8 7 6 5 4 3 2

TABLE OF CONTENTS

—᭟᭟—

PART ONE
WE BECOME WHAT WE CELEBRATE

—᭟᭟—

—⁓—

PART THREE
THE SEVEN PILLARS OF CATHOLIC SPIRITUALITY

—⁓—

Imagine this...

You're driving home from work next Monday after a long day. You tune in your radio. You hear a blurb about a little village in India where some villagers have died suddenly, strangely, of a flu that has never been seen before. It's not influenza, but three or four people are dead, and it's kind of interesting, and they are sending some doctors over there to investigate it. You don't think much about it, but coming home from church on Sunday you hear another radio spot. Only they say it's not three villagers, it's 30,000 villagers in the back hills of this particular area of India, and it's on TV that night. CNN runs a little blurb: people are heading there from the disease center in Atlanta because this disease strain has never been seen before.

By Monday morning when you get up, it's the lead story. It's not just India; it's Pakistan, Afghanistan, Iran, and before you know it, you're hearing this story everywhere, and they have now coined it as "the mystery flu." The President has made some comment that he and his family are praying and hoping that all will go well over there. But everyone is wondering, "How are we going to contain it?"

That's when the President of France makes an announcement that shocks Europe. He is closing their borders. No flights from India, Pakistan, or any of the countries where this thing has been seen. And that's why that night you are watching a little bit of CNN before going to bed. Your jaw hits your chest when a weeping woman is translated into English from a French news program. There's a man lying in a hospital in Paris, dying of the mystery flu. It has come to Europe.

Panic strikes. As best they can tell, after contracting the disease, you have it for a week before you even know it. Then you have four days of unbelievable symptoms. And then you die. Britain closes its borders, but it's too late. South Hampton, Liverpool, North Hampton, and it's Tuesday morning when the President of the United States makes the following announcement: "Due to a national-security risk, all flights to and from Europe and Asia have been canceled. If your loved ones are overseas, I'm sorry. They cannot come back until we find a cure for this thing."

Within four days, our nation has been plunged into an unbelievable fear. People are wondering, "What if it comes to this country?" And preachers on Tuesday are saying it's the scourge of God. It's Wednesday night, and you are at a church prayer meeting when somebody runs in from the parking lot and yells, "Turn on a radio, turn on a radio!" And while everyone in church listens to a little transistor radio with a microphone stuck up to it, the announcement is made. Two women are lying in a Long Island hospital, dying from the mystery flu. Within hours it seems, the disease envelops the country.

People are working around the clock, trying to find an antidote. Nothing is working. California, Oregon, Arizona, Florida, Massachusetts. It's as though it's just sweeping in from the borders.

And then all of a sudden the news comes out. The code has been broken. A cure can be found. A vaccine can be made. It's going to take the blood of somebody who hasn't been infected, and so, sure enough, all through the Midwest, through all those channels of emergency broadcasting, everyone is asked to do one simple thing: Go to your downtown hospital and have your blood analyzed. That's all we ask of you. When you hear the sirens go off in your neighborhood, please make your way quickly, quietly, and safely to the hospitals.

Sure enough, when you and your family get down there late on that Friday night, there is a long line, and they've got nurses and doctors coming out and pricking fingers and taking blood and putting labels on it. Your spouse and your kids are out there, and they take your blood and say, "Wait here in the parking lot, and if we call your name, you can be dismissed and go home." You stand around, scared, with your neighbors, wondering what on earth is going on, and if this is the end of the world.

Suddenly, a young man comes running out of the hospital screaming. He's yelling a name and waving a clipboard. What? He yells it again! And your son tugs on your jacket and says, "Daddy, that's me." Before you know it, they have grabbed your boy. "Wait a minute. Hold on!" And they say, "It's okay, his blood is clean. His blood is pure. We want to make sure he doesn't have the disease. We think he has the right blood type."

Five tense minutes later, out come the doctors and nurses crying and hugging one another - some are even laughing. It's the first time you have seen anybody laugh in a week, and an old doctor walks up to you and says, "Thank you, sir. Your son's blood is perfect. It's clean, it is pure, and we can make the vaccine."

As the word begins to spread all across that parking lot full of folks, people are screaming and praying and laughing and crying. But then the gray-haired doctor pulls you and your wife aside and says, "May we see you for a moment? We didn't realize that the donor would be a minor and we... we need you to sign a consent form."

You begin to sign, and then you see that the box for the number of pints of blood to be taken is empty. "H-h-h-how many pints?" And that is when the old doctor's smile fades, and he says, "We had no idea it would be a little child. We weren't prepared. We need it all!" "But... but . . . I don't understand. He's my only son!" "We are talking about the whole world here. Please sign. We... we... need to hurry!"

"But can't you give him a transfusion?" "If we had clean blood we would. Please, will you please sign?"

In numb silence you do. Then they say, "Would you like to have a moment with him before we begin?"

Could you walk back? Could you walk back to that room where he sits on a table saying, "Daddy? Mommy? What's going on?" Could you take his hands and say, "Son, your mommy and I love you, and we would never, ever let anything happen to you that didn't just have to be! Do you understand that?" And when that old doctor comes back in and says, "I'm sorry, we've got to get started. People all over the world are dying," could you leave? Could you walk out while he is saying, "Dad? Mom? Dad? Why . . . why have you abandoned me?"

And then next week, when they have the ceremony to honor your son, and some folks sleep through it, and some folks don't even bother to come because they have better things to do, and some folks come with a pretentious smile and just pretend to care, would you want to jump up and say, "EXCUSE ME! MY SON DIED FOR YOU! DON'T YOU EVEN CARE? DOES IT MEAN NOTHING TO YOU?"

I wonder, is that what God wants to say? "MY SON DIED FOR YOU! DOES IT MEAN NOTHING? DON'T YOU KNOW HOW MUCH I CARE?"

—◦◦◦—

Father, seeing it from your eyes should break our hearts. Maybe now we can begin to comprehend the great love you have for us.

REDISCOVERING

CATHOLICISM

The Church, like so many other things in life, is not something we inherit from generations past or take over from our predecessors. The Church is on loan to us from future generations.

PART ONE

WE BECOME WHAT
WE CELEBRATE

Two thousand years ago, a very small group of people captured the attention and fascinated the imaginations of the entire western world. At first, they were thought to be of no consequence, the followers of a man most people considered to be nothing more than an itinerant preacher. But when this man was put to death, a dozen of his followers rose up and began telling people about his life and teachings. They began telling his story. They were uneducated men who had no social status, no money, and no worldly authority; and yet, from the very beginning, people were joining this quiet revolutionary group a hundred at a time. As their popularity soared, the prevailing authorities grew fearful of their power, just as they had been afraid of their leader. In some places, the authorities tried to put an end to this new group by randomly killing some of its members, but those chosen considered it the highest honor to die for what they believed. This only intrigued the hearts and perplexed the minds of the people even more.

This small group of people were the first Christians. They were the original followers of Jesus of Nazareth and the first members of what we know today as the Catholic Church.

As the centuries have passed, much has changed. Today, Catholicism is the largest faith community in the world with more than 1.2 billion members. In every time and place for two thousand years, the Catholic Church has fed, clothed, and housed more people in need than any other group or institution in history. The Church was responsible for the birth of both the education system and the health care system that stand as pillars in our modern society. Throughout the centuries, the Church has also been the largest benefactor of the arts, nurturing these elements of cultural life that have the ability to elevate the human heart, mind, and spirit so effortlessly to the things of God. Today, the Church is the largest landowner in the world, owning land in almost every community from the most remote and rural locations to the most sophisticated cities. In this modern day and age, the Catholic Church remains the world's premier institutional defender of human rights.

And yet, as great as our achievements may be, as great as our numbers are today, we seem unable to capture the attention and intrigue the imaginations of people the way our spiritual ancestors did.

The story of Jesus Christ is the most powerful story in history and has directly or indirectly influenced every noble aspect of our modern civilization. But amidst the hustle and bustle of our daily lives, it is easy to become distracted and distance ourselves from this story. From time to time, someone comes along who reminds us of the spellbinding power the Gospel has when it is actually lived. There is something ultimately attractive about men and women *striving* to become the-best-version-of-themselves. It is this *striving* that we need to rediscover as a Church. We have become too comfortably a part of the modern secular culture, and this comfort has resulted in a complacency toward the life-giving words of the Gospel. Too often, we listen to these words but do not allow them to transform our hearts and our lives.

I pray with all my heart that we can collectively rediscover what it means to live a Christian life. And with this knowledge, I hope we can embrace this *striving* that causes the human person to thrive and bloom. If we can get that *striving* back, we will once again capture the attention and intrigue the imaginations of all people everywhere.

CHAPTER ONE

OUR UNIVERSAL HUNGER

Throughout human history, there has never been a shortage of men and women willing to point humanity along the right path. Nor have the needs of the human family ever been a secret: food, shelter, purposeful work, companionship, freedom, forgiveness, acceptance, and love. In every age, there is an abundance of people who are able to articulate the truth of these matters and announce their social implications particular to that time. These people stand at the crossroads and point humanity down a path they have never traveled themselves. In our own age, there is certainly no shortage of books, tapes, courses, radio shows, seminars, retreats, and television programs – all of which speak to these needs in various ways.

But amidst this abundance, there is a great poverty. It seems in every place and in every time, the shortage is always of men and women willing to *lead* humanity along the right path with the example of their own lives. In each moment of history, authentic lives are ever so rare.

Appearance vs. The Authentic

Our own age seems to be governed by illusion and deception. We have built a whole culture based on appearance. Everything looks good, but scratch just below the surface, and you will discover little substance. Appearance has become a standard. We have grown so numb to the realities of good and evil that lying and cheating have become almost universally accepted as necessary evils. So we tolerate them, as long as they are performed in the dim light of "respectability." Occasionally, in the midst of this cultural darkness, the great light of the human spirit shines forth with honesty and integrity. At those times we seem surprised, even taken off-guard. Honesty, loyalty, and integrity seem almost out of place in the modern schema.

But beneath the surface, under the guise of appearances, this age like any other is made up of people like you and me. And if you listen carefully, if you look closely, you will discover that the people are hungry. Created to love and be loved, we feel a restlessness, a longing for more, a profound discontent with our lives and with our culture. Our hunger is not for appearances, but for something of substance. We are hungry for truth. The people of today are starving for the authentic, thirsting for the tiniest droplet of sincerity, aching to experience the genuine.

Why Has Christianity Been Rejected?

At this same time, Christianity has been largely rejected. There are many people who faithfully attend church each Sunday, but increasing numbers are choosing not to come to church. This is particularly true among younger generations.

Those of us who call ourselves Christian do so because we believe that the life and teachings of Jesus Christ are the personification of truth, sincerity, and authenticity. If this belief is correct, if the people of this age really are hungering for truth, sincerity, and authenticity, then as Christians we must ask ourselves, Why are they not enthusiastically embracing Christianity? Why, in fact, are so many people so hostile toward Christ and his Church?

I sense it is because the people of today believe that Christians, Christianity, and perhaps Catholics in particular, are as much a part of this culture of appearance and deception as anyone else. Their desire for truth has not diminished, but people have become wary, doubtful, skeptical, and sadly, even cynical in their search for truth. And to be honest, I cannot blame them for their attitude. I do not agree with their position, but I understand it. And perhaps more importantly, I can see how they arrived at that place of philosophical confusion and theological desolation.

The cause of much of this confusion is the unprecedented proliferation of words, symbols, images, and every manner of communication in the latter part of the twentieth century. People are tired; they are worn out, overloaded with information, and overwhelmed with the social, political, and economic climate. They are not *striving* to thrive, they are merely trying to survive. This is a tired culture.

The Cry for Help

More than ever, non-Christians and non-practicing Christians are sending you, me, and all of Christianity a message. Though they are not aware of it, they are indirectly giving witness to the Gospel. For within the message, there is a profound challenge for you and me to embrace a life rooted more fully in the example and teachings of Jesus Christ. Their message is clear, unmistakable, and disarmingly simple. Our siblings, parents, and children are sending us this message, as are our friends, neighbors, and colleagues. They are saying, whispering, crying out, "Don't tell me, show me!"

Their plea comes from a longing deep within them and represents their great hunger. They don't want to see another television evangelist, they don't want to read another book or hear another tape about Christianity, and they don't want to hear your amazing story of conversion. They want the real thing. They want to witness someone, any-one - just one will do — living an authentic life. Someone whose words are spoken by the authori-ty of his or her actions. Someone striving humbly but heroically to live by what is good, true, and noble in the midst of and in spite of this modern climate.

They are not sending us this message merely to sound the childish cry of "hypocrite." Rather, theirs is a natural cry — a cry for help. They are saying to us, "Don't tell me, show me!" because they are so hungry for a courageous example of the authentic life, a life lived to the fullest, in this day and age. Seeing the conflicts and contradic-tions of our lives, they cry "hypocrite" out of their hurt and anger, because the disappointment of dis-covering that we are not living the life we espouse robs them of their own hope to live an authentic life. They are calling out to us like sheep without a shepherd, wanting to be fed, wanting to be led to the pastures of kindness, compassion, generosi-ty, forgiveness, acceptance, freedom, and love.

I have heard this cry a thousand times, but the words of one man echo in my mind like a bad dream that keeps returning to haunt a terrified child. They are the words of Mahatma Gandhi. He is a man for whom I have great admiration - a man whom I believe strove with all his might to live an authentic life. I have studied his life and writings extensively, but one passage stands out. It speaks to me with a clarity that pierces my heart.

In relation to the well known fact that Gandhi read from the New Testament everyday and often quoted the Christian Scriptures, a reporter once asked him why he had never become a Christian. He answered, "If I had ever met one, I would have become one." In his own way, Gandhi was saying, "Don't tell me, show me!" and simultaneously revealing his yearning for an example of an authentic life.

With all this being said, I believe there is also a desire within each of us to live an authentic life. We desire not only to witness authentic lives, but also to live an authentic life ourselves. We genuinely want to be true to ourselves and true to God. At times, we have perhaps resolved to live such a life with all the fervor we could muster. But, distracted by the sweet seduction of pleasure, possessions, or power, we have wandered from the narrow path. We know the truth, but we lack the discipline and strength of character to align the actions of our lives with that truth (cf. Matthew 26:41). We have given ourselves over to a thousand different whims, cravings, and fantasies. Our lives have become merely a distortion of the truth we know and profess. We know the human family's need for kindness, compassion, generosity, forgiveness, acceptance, freedom, and love, but we have divided our hearts with a thousand contradictions and compromises.

At every moment, the entire modern world kneels before us, begging, pleading, beckoning, for some brave man or woman to come forward and lead them by example of an authentic life.

Amidst the abundance of this age, which at times may seem all-prevailing, there is a great hunger in the people of today. We have a universal hunger for the authentic.

CHAPTER TWO

THE PREVAILING PHILOSOPHY

Every culture is the fruit of the ideas and attitudes of its people. These ideas and attitudes come together in both people and cultures to form philosophies. Our own age is one of great philosophical poverty, and as a result, we live in an age of tremendous moral and ethical confusion.

We each have our own philosophy. This philosophy is comprised of a set of beliefs by which we choose to live. These beliefs are probably many and varied. A person might believe that there is one God, that the earth is round, and that you should never go anywhere without an umbrella.

These beliefs are very different, but could co-exist within a person's personal philosophy. A philosophy is a rule of life.

What's your philosophy?

While we may not be able to articulate clearly our personal philosophy, we call upon this "rule of life" many times each day. Everyday we make hundreds of decisions. Some of these decisions affect what we eat and what we wear, while others affect the very direction of our lives. In every case, these decisions are determined by our personal philosophy.

The philosophical environment of a community is made up of the collective philosophies of the people who make up that community. A community could be as small as a family or as large as a nation. In the present age, there are certain philosophical trends that are governing the decision process. I find these trends disturbing on many levels. They disturb me as a human being. They disturb me as a brother, son, and member of a family. They disturb me as a citizen of a modern nation. They disturb me as a person of faith and as a Christian. And ultimately, they disturb me as a Catholic, as a believing member of the one, holy, catholic, and apostolic Church.

Although there are many philosophies influencing the modern schema, I would like to propose that there are three major practical philosophies upon which we have constructed our modern culture. I will leave it to the reader to decide whether we have built our culture on rock like the wise man, or on sand like the fool (cf. Matthew 7:24-27).

Individualism

When faced with a decision, "What's in it for me?" is the question that seems to dominate the inner dialogue of most people today. This question is the creed of the philosophy we call *Individualism*, which is based on an ultimate concern for self. In the present climate, the most dominant trend governing the decision-making process, and therefore the formation of our cultural belief system, is Individualism.

No community, whether it is as small as a family or as large as a nation, can grow strong by this attitude. Individualism always weakens the community and causes the whole to suffer. In every instance, Individualism is a cancerous growth.

The social and political reforms of our age have exulted the individual in a way that is unhealthy for society as a whole. Under the pressure and guidance of a number of special interest groups that represent only a fraction of society at large, the rights of the individual have been gradually elevated and ultimately placed above the rights of society as a whole. A perfect example is the recent situation in California, where a court banned public schools from using "under God" when saying the Pledge of Allegiance. The rights of the individual have been strengthened at all costs, with no regard for right and wrong. At the same time, everything has been done to weaken the rights of the Church, the State, and authority of any type.

All this has been done under the banner of false freedom. The false and adolescent notion is that freedom is the opportunity to do whatever you want, wherever you want, whenever you want, without the interference of any other person or party. This is not freedom.

Our culture places a very high premium on self-expression, but is relatively disinterested in producing "selves" that are worth expressing.

The fruits of Individualism are no secret to any of us: greed, selfishness, and exploitation. What would become of a family or a nation in which each member adopted Individualism as his or her own personal philosophy?

Hedonism

This naked Individualism is only furthered by the present generations' assertion that pleasure is the supreme good. This assertion unmasks *Hedonism* as the second philosophical mark of our age. Hedonism is the philosophy that places pleasure as the ultimate goal and aim of life. The motto, the creed, the catch-cry of the Hedonist is, "If it feels good, do it!"

Under the guise of a supposedly "newfound freedom," this ancient imposter has seduced and deceived present generations. This is the great paradox regarding the philosophical marks of our age. The people who promote and propagate them represent them as new and different, but if we undress these philosophies, we quickly discover that the present cultural environment is based on ideologies of the past. We mistakenly believe that these philosophies are new and different. If we look a little further, we will discover that the cultures that first employed these ideas, or have since adopted them, can all trace their decline to these philosophies.

Whenever Hedonism has emerged as a dominant practical philosophy in other cultures and sub-cultures, it has always produced men and women who were lazy, lustful, and gluttonous. Furthermore, Hedonism has been a contributing factor to the demise of every culture and sub-culture it has featured in significantly. The Roman Empire is a perfect example.

Hedonism is not an expression of freedom, it is a passport to the enslavement of a thousand addictions. And the end it produces is not pleasure, but despair.

Minimalism

The third philosophical mark of our age perfectly complements the greed of Individualism and the lust of Hedonism in the demise of human character. Accompanying these other modern creeds, "What's in it for me?" and "If it feels good, do it!" is the creed of *Minimalism*. The minimalist is always asking, "What is the least I can do...?"

A minimalist is always seeking to exert the minimum effort and receive the maximum reward. Minimalism is the enemy of excellence and the father of mediocrity. It is one of the greatest philosophical diseases of our age. Minimalism has infected every aspect of our lives and society, and tragically, it is also one of the philosophical diseases that is eating away at the Church.

Consciously or sub-consciously, people everywhere seem to be asking, "What is the least I can do and still keep my job? What is the least I can do and still get reasonable grades in school? What is the least I can do and still keep my marriage alive? What is the least I can do and still stay physically fit? What is the least I can do and still get to Heaven? What is the least I can do...?"

—⁓—

It is within the philosophical realms of *Individualism*, *Hedonism*, and *Minimalism,* that most people make the majority of their decisions everyday. These philosophies are being communicated powerfully yet subtly, via every social, cultural, and political medium. Through movies and music, literature and fashion, government policy and education, these philosophies have nudged their way into every aspect of our lives. It didn't happen overnight; it has taken decades. We would have reacted if it had happened overnight, just as a frog will jump straight out if you drop it in a pot of boiling hot water. But if you put a frog in a pot of cold water and then slowly raise the temperature, it will stay in the pot even to its death.

With all this in mind, we shouldn't be surprised by the radical increase in sexual promiscuity and sex crimes today, or by the cultural manipulation and destruction of the family unit, or by the gradual but persistent political undermining of family values in our modern societies. It shouldn't surprise us that corporate and political fraud have escalated at alarming rates. Truth be known, we shouldn't be surprised that, during my short lifetime, more than six times the number of people murdered in the atrocity we call the Holocaust have fallen victim to abortion in the United States alone. Teenagers walking into classrooms and shooting students and teachers, children killing their parents, and the dramatic and unprecedented increase in non-warfare violence shouldn't shock us. These are the signs of the times, and they are merely the fruits of the philosophies that mark this moment in history.

Any community that adopts these philosophies, whether that community is as small as a family or as large as a nation, does so at its own peril. A philosophy is a way of life. Individualism, Hedonism, and Minimalism will destroy every individual and community that practices them. They are ultimately self-destructive philosophies.

—*⁂*—

The crisis of the modern world is a crisis of ideas. Thought determines action. Ideas shape our lives. It would not be too soon for us to learn that ideas have consequences.

CHAPTER THREE

IS JESUS STILL RELEVANT?

It also should come as no surprise to us that, in this modern environment, the relevance of Jesus is being seriously questioned. The reason is simple. The philosophy of Christ is very different from the prevailing philosophies of our modern culture. In fact, they are completely opposed to each other. And yet, the teachings of Christ and these modern philosophies both claim to be the key to the fulfillment of a yearning that is common to us all.

Our Quest for Happiness

The human heart is on a quest for happiness. Every human heart yearns for happiness like the desert yearns for rain. You have a desire for happiness, I have a desire for happiness. This desire is universal, common to every member of the human family. We simply desire to be happy, and we act from this desire.

We often do things that we think will make us happy, but which in fact end up making us miserable. Under the influence of philosophies such as Individualism, Hedonism, and Minimalism, we often seek the happiness we desire through pleasure, possessions, power, and the path of least resistance. Each of these may offer moments of happiness, but they end too soon, having lasted ever so briefly, and our quest for a lasting happiness continues. These moments of happiness are of course real, but only as real as a shadow. The shadow of a person is real, but it is nothing compared to the actual person. So many of us spend a large portion of our lives chasing shadows.

The modern search for happiness is governed by Individualism, Hedonism, Minimalism and their fruits: greed, lust, laziness, gluttony, selfishness, exploitation, and deception. And yet, as these philosophies become more and more the focus of modern lifestyles, people seem to be filled with a greater discontent and unhappiness with each passing day.

Is it possible that these philosophies cannot deliver what they promise? Is it possible that there is something lacking in these philosophies that makes it impossible for the human person to find happiness through them?

God & Happiness

I believe God wants us to be happy. I believe God gave us the yearning for happiness that constantly preoccupies our human hearts. It is as if God placed this yearning within each human heart as a spiritual navigational instrument designed to reunite us with our destiny. As a Father who takes a sincere and active interest in the lives of his children, God sent his only Son to respond to humanity's yearning for happiness, and to offer direction in satisfying that yearning. After all, God himself is the author of our yearning for happiness.

The philosophy of Christ is the ultimate philosophy of human happiness. At the same time, the philosophy of Christ is one of self-donation. This is the great paradox of God's teaching. In our misguided adventures, we may catch glimpses of happiness living outside of the philosophy of Christ. You may even taste happiness for a moment living a life contrary to the philosophy of Christ, but these are stolen moments. They may seem real, but they are just shadows of something infinitely greater.

The Attitude of Christ

Jesus never asked, "What's in it for me?" He was not motivated by the Individualist creed; he was motivated by a spirit of service. Far from advocating a Hedonistic deification of pleasure, Jesus gently proclaimed a life of self-denial, saying, "Whoever wishes to follow me, let him deny himself and take up his cross" (Matthew 16:24). He certainly didn't ask himself, "What is the least I can do and still bring salvation to humanity?" No, he asked, "What is the most I can do?" For this is the question of the lover. The attitude of Christ forms a stark contrast to the philosophies of Individualism, Hedonism, and Minimalism.

The life that Jesus invites us to live is very different than the lifestyle our modern culture invites us to live. Individualism, Hedonism, Minimalism - and their various sundry ally philosophies such as Relativism and Materialism - encourage us to do whatever we want, wherever we want, whenever we want. On the other hand, Jesus invites us to a life of discipline.

Having appeared to Mary Magdalene after his Resurrection, Jesus summoned the disciples to Galilee. When the eleven were gathered together on the mountain, Jesus said, "Go therefore and make disciples of every nation" (Matthew 28:19). Jesus did not say, "Go and make followers of every nation."

It is easy to be a follower, but to be a disciple requires discipline. Christ invites us to a life of discipline not for his sake, but for our sake; not to help him, but to help us; not to make him happy, but to allow us to share in his happiness.

The Role of Discipline

Jesus said, "I have come that you may have life and have it to the fullest" (John 10:10). The path that leads to "fullness of life" is discipline. There are four major aspects of the human person — physical, emotional, intellectual, and spiritual. When we eat well, exercise often, and sleep regularly, we feel more fully alive physically. When we love, when we give priority to the significant relationships of our lives, when we give of ourselves to help others in their journey, we feel more fully alive emotionally. When we study, we feel more fully alive intellectually. When we come before God in prayer, openly and honestly, we experience life more fully spiritually. All of these life-giving endeavors require discipline. When are we most fully alive? When we embrace a life of discipline. The human person thrives on discipline.

Are you thriving? Or are you just surviving?

Discipline awakens us from our philosophical stupor and refines every aspect of the human person. Discipline doesn't enslave or stifle the human person; rather, it sets us free to soar to unimagined heights. Discipline sharpens the human senses, allowing us to savor the subtler tastes of life's experiences. Whether those experiences are physical, emotional, intellectual, or spiritual, discipline elevates them to their ultimate reality. Discipline heightens every human experience and increases every human ability. The life and teachings of Jesus Christ invite us to embrace this life-giving discipline.

—⁂—

Many people consider Jesus irrelevant today because he proposes a life of discipline. Is discipline then to be considered the core of Jesus' philosophy? No. Christ proposes a life of discipline not for its own sake, and certainly not to stifle or control us; rather, he proposes discipline as the key to freedom.

In the midst of the complexities of this modern era, we find ourselves enslaved and imprisoned by a thousand different whims, cravings, addictions, and attachments. We have subscribed to the adolescent notion that freedom is the ability to do whatever you want, wherever you want, whenever you want, without interference from any authority. Could the insanity of our modern philosophy be any more apparent? Freedom is not the ability to do whatever you want. Freedom is the strength of character to do what is good, true, noble, and right. Freedom without discipline is impossible.

Is freedom then to be considered the core of Jesus' philosophy? No. What then, is the core of his philosophy? Well, as it turns out, the people of his own time were curious for an answer to this very question.

One day, while Jesus was teaching a large group of people in the synagogue, a man asked Our Lord a question from his position in the multitude. He was a learned man, one of those doctors of the law who were no longer able to understand the teaching revealed to Moses because it had become so twisted and entangled in the ways of men. He questioned Our Lord, saying, "Teacher, which is the greatest of the Commandments?"

Jesus opened his divine lips slowly, with the calm assurance of somebody who knows what he is talking about and replied, "You shall love the Lord your God with your whole heart, your whole mind, and your whole soul. This is the first and the greatest of the Commandments. And the second is like it, you shall love your neighbor as yourself. Upon these two rest the whole law and all the prophets" (Matthew 22:34-40).

Love is the core of Jesus' philosophy. But, in order to love you must be free. For to love is to give your *self* freely and without reservation. Yet, to give your *self* - to another person, to an endeavor, or to God - you must first possess your *self*. This possession of *self* is freedom. It is a prerequisite for love, and is attained only through discipline.

Jesus in History

Before Christmas last year, I saw a Jewish scholar interviewed on television. The topic of discussion was the influence Jesus has exerted on human history. In summary, the scholar concluded, "The impact this man has had on human history is undeniable. Because of this man we call Jesus, the world will never again be the same. Because of Jesus, men and women will never think the same. Regardless of whether or not we believe he was the Son of God, because of this man who walked the earth two thousand years ago, men and women will never live the same, will never be the same."

Sometimes, in this turbulent cultural environment, which can be particularly anti-Christian, we can lose sight of the impact Christ has had on history. Caught up in the day-to-day challenges of our busy lives, it is sometimes easy to forget the unfathomable influence this one man has had.

—◈—

There are a great many people today who think that Jesus is irrelevant in the modern context. I suspect these people are suffering from a modern madness caused by an ignorance of self and history. As we get to know ourselves, our deepest needs, and the history of humanity, the relevance of Jesus Christ to modern man becomes startlingly clear.

Is Jesus still relevant?

Gather all the books that have been written about the life and teachings of Jesus. Add to them all the artwork Christian life has inspired. Now consider all the music inspired by Christ. Not to be forgotten is the fact that the Church nurtured and nourished the development of the arts for centuries. Christianity was the moral foundation upon which America and many other nations built themselves. Now consider the fact that prior to Christ walking the earth, there was never any such thing as a hospital. Where were the sick when Jesus walked the earth? They were on the side of the road, left there to rot and die by relatives who feared for their own health. How is it that we have also collectively forgotten that until the Church introduced education for the masses, there was never any such thing as an education for the common man? Education was only for the elite until the Church recognized and proclaimed the dignity of every human person and introduced education for the masses.

All of these represent aspects of the measurable impact Christ has had on human history. And yet, these are all just dim reflections of the person who was and is Jesus Christ. Adding all of these together is still nothing compared to the impact Christ can have on your life, on my life. All the worldly success of Christ and the Church are insignificant compared to the change Christ can effect in your heart, in my heart.

The life of Jesus Christ is indelibly engraved upon history, neither the erosion of time nor the devastating and compounding effects of evil have been able to erase his influence. Some people thought he was crazy, others considered him a misfit, a troublemaker, a rebel. He was condemned as a criminal, and yet, his life and teachings echo and reverberate throughout history. He saw things differently, and he had no respect for the status quo. You can praise him, disagree with him, quote him, disbelieve him, glorify him, or vilify him.

About the only thing you cannot do is ignore him, and that is a lesson that every age learns in its own way.

You can't ignore Jesus because he changed things. He is the single greatest agent of change in human history. He made the lame walk, taught the simple, set captives free, gave sight to the blind, fed the hungry, healed the sick, comforted the afflicted, afflicted the comfortable, and in all of these, captured the imaginations of every generation.

His teachings are not complex or exclusive, but simple and applicable to everyone, everywhere, in every time in history, regardless of age, color, or state in life. Beyond life's complexities, there is simplicity. Beneath life's confusion, there is understanding. It is the Gospel, the Good News. Within it, through it, we find salvation. And I believe that part of that salvation is happiness - not the foolish, empty happiness that this modern age associates with getting what you want. It is a happiness deeper and higher than any happiness we could imagine or design for ourselves.

Christ came to reconcile us with the Father, and in doing so, offered the satisfaction of this craving for happiness that preoccupies our human hearts. Love is our origin and our destiny. Our yearning for happiness is a yearning for love. Created to love and be loved, we seek out the fulfillment of our purpose. "God is love" (1 John 4:8), and our yearning for happiness is ultimately a yearning for God. *The Catechism of the Catholic Church* wastes no time in addressing this truth. The opening point of Chapter One, Section One, reads, "The desire for God is written in the human heart, because man is created by God and for God; and God never ceases to draw man to himself. Only in God will man find the truth and happiness he never stops yearning for."

Our desire for happiness is not going to go away. It is part of the human condition. Our quest for happiness is a quest for God. This is the genius of God. Our yearning for happiness is the ultimate and eternal homing device, designed to draw us gently toward our eternal home. Our yearning for happiness is a yearning for union with our Creator. As Augustine pointed out so simply and eloquently, "Our hearts are restless until they rest in you, Lord." Wherever men and women yearn for happiness, Christ will be relevant. He alone is the fulfillment and satisfaction of this yearning, and so for every person in every place and time he remains, "the Way, the Truth, and the Life" (John 14:6).

CHAPTER FOUR

SEARCHING FOR IDENTITY

Today, perhaps more than ever before, we are struggling as Catholics to establish a positive identity in society. What has caused this identity crisis? How do we establish a vibrant identity for Catholicism in the modern world?

The Mission

The cultural settings of different ages may change, and change dramatically, but two things remain the same in every place and in every time: the human heart's yearning for happiness and the mission of the Church. In fact, the mission of the Church is God's direct and intimate response to the human heart's unceasing yearning for happiness.

At the dawn of this new millennium, it is essential that we remind ourselves that Christ did not entrust the Church with a political, social, or economic mission, but with a mission that is primarily spiritual. The mission of the Church is to proclaim the Gospel to the people of every nation in every age (cf. Mark 16:15). At the same time, as we live out this mission, it can and should impact the political, social, and economic order of the societies in which Christians live. When the Gospel is applied to the daily activities of our lives, it elevates every honest human endeavor and every aspect of society. The Gospel is alive and active. It has the power to transform our lives, our communities, our nations, and indeed the whole world.

The Adventure of Salvation

Once we are aware of our yearning for happiness, the adventure of salvation begins. Our yearning for happiness is God's invitation to join this adventure. God has a plan of salvation for each of us. Your adventure of salvation is unique and different than mine. In *The Rhythm of Life*, I wrote extensively about the relationship between our legitimate needs, our deepest desires, and our talents. I believe it is through this relationship that God reveals to us our unique path of salvation. Francis of Assisi walked a different path than Teresa of Avila. The paths were different, but the result was the same.

When God created us, he created us with legitimate needs. We all have legitimate physical, emotional, intellectual, and spiritual needs. To eat is a legitimate need. If we do not eat, we will die. When we hear these legitimate needs calling to us, we hear the voice of God, for it is he who gave us these needs. Similarly, our hearts are filled with desires. The good desires that fill our hearts are placed there by God to call us along the path of salvation. One of the most ancient practices of Christian spirituality is the unveiling of the deepest desires of our hearts. When we hear these deepest desires calling us forth, we hear the voice of God. Finally, in creating us, God endowed us each with certain talents and abilities. When we hear these talents calling us forth we hear the voice of God, again inviting us to participate fully in the adventure of salvation.

It is through prayer, reflection, the Scriptures, the grace of the sacraments, and the guidance of the Church, that we discover and walk the path that God is calling us to walk. In our own way, we all seek out our individual destiny. Drawn by our yearning for happiness, we may seek to experience pleasure, possessions, and even power, but the world and all it has to offer can never content the human heart. God alone can satisfy the deepest cravings of our hearts. It is the task of the Church to introduce us to our destiny by opening up to us the mystery of God, who is our ultimate end and our destiny.

By embracing the adventure of salvation, we become with each passing effort more perfectly the persons we were created to be. Christ has commissioned the Church to guide and direct each of us individually along this path. Our dialogue and interaction with the Church is designed to help us become the-best-version-of-ourselves. It is for this reason that in every age the Church proclaims the unchanging truths of the life and teachings of Jesus Christ – the Gospel. In doing so, she invites us to a life of discipline.

There are certain disciplines that are associated with the life of an athlete. An athlete abides by a certain diet and adheres to a certain training regimen. Athletes don't stay out all night partying because they know they have to wake early the next morning for training. All these are part of an athlete's lifestyle. So it is with the life of a Christian. There are disciplines and practices that must be adhered to and abided by if we are to walk faithfully along the path of salvation, fulfill our destiny, and enjoy the happiness with which God wants to fill us. Discipline is an integral part of the adventure of salvation.

Catholics Today

If we had to narrow it down, what would be the one great difference between the first Christians and Catholics today? This is a difficult question. Some may say it is impossible to answer such a question, but as I have traveled the world in the past seven years, visiting the Church in more than forty countries, the answer has become almost self-evident.

For the first Christians, Christianity was a lifestyle. The first Christians shared a common life. Living in community, they often worked together, prayed together, and studied the Scriptures together. Their faith was the center of their lives and it affected everything they did. They shared meals together, played together, and cared for each other in sickness. They strove earnestly to apply the guiding principles of the Gospel to each activity in their lives. They comforted each other in their afflictions and challenged each other to live the Gospel more fully. There was unity and continuity between their professional lives and their family lives, between their social lives and their lives as members of the Church. Then, at the pinnacle of their common life, they celebrated Eucharist together.

Today, amidst the busyness and complexities of modern life, the great majority of Catholics are challenged merely to make it to Mass each Sunday. In modern society, a great separation has taken place between the various aspects of our lives. Many people feel that they need to leave the values and principles of their faith outside of certain activities in the same way they leave a coat in a waiting room. The modern world tries to separate faith from reason, the professional from the personal, the means from the ends. This separationalist approach destroys "unity of life" and creates the modern madness of feeling torn in two.

Catholicism Is a Lifestyle

It is equally important at this time in history that we ask, "What is Catholicism?" and "What does it mean to be Catholic?"

Catholicism is not merely a religion, or a sect, or a set of rules. When small minds and smaller spirits try to capture the essence of Catholicism, this is often what they tend to conclude. But no, Catholicism is more than a religion. Catholicism is not just another movement. It is more than a set of lifeless rules and regulations. The essence of Catholicism is not sin, punishment, duty, or obligation.

The essence of Catholicism is transformation. You cannot become more like Jesus Christ and at the same time stay as you are. To be Catholic means to be striving to live the Gospel, to be striving to become more like Jesus Christ. It is this dynamic approach to transformation that animates the human person – physically, emotionally, intellectually, and spiritually - and allows us to experience life "to the fullest" (John 10:10).

Catholicism is a dynamic way of life that encourages and empowers each individual to become the-best-version-of-themselves. This lifestyle promotes self-integration by taking into account every aspect of the human person. And as each soul journeys toward its individual destiny, God employs that soul to touch others, to serve others, and to inspire others to make their own journey. Catholicism is a way of life in which the giving and receiving go on in equal measure. Catholicism nurtures the self and the community. Catholicism affects every area of our lives and is a guiding light in all of our decisions. It is both the philosophical and theological base and the practical inspiration. Catholicism is a call to live an authentic life. When embraced as a lifestyle, Catholicism causes the elevation of every human activity. Catholicism provides the template and the tools for bringing each soul into harmony with God, self, and others.

Identity Crisis

In the midst of a tumultuous and rapidly changing cultural environment, we have struggled as Catholics to establish a vibrant identity in the present age. Plagued and persecuted by false stereotypes, we have failed to establish an authentic Catholic identity in the modern world. As Catholics at the dawn of the twenty-first century, we are in the midst of a serious identity crisis.

From where will we draw the guidance and inspiration to re-establish a vibrant Catholic identity in the world? At supper with his disciples for the last time, Jesus himself offered an answer to this question. His words are as fresh and relevant today as they were twenty centuries ago: "I give you a new commandment: love one another. As I have loved you, so you should also love one another. This is how all will know that you are my disciples, if you have love for one another" (John 13:34-35).

How I wish that when people discovered you are Catholic, they could immediately conclude that you are honest, hardworking, generous, loving, joyful, compassionate, temperate, humble, disciplined, prayerful, and generally in love with life. You wouldn't need too many people like this to develop a positive reputation for Catholicism in a local community. I pray that God raises them up. I pray that God will transform you and me into Catholics of that caliber.

CHAPTER FIVE

WHAT ARE WE CELEBRATING?

As I have traveled the world, I have learned that every faith community has problems and issues. Every Catholic diocese and parish in the world has difficulties. In some places, I have seen these problems and issues drain communities of energy and enthusiasm, causing division and resentment. In other places, these difficulties have given birth to renewed energy and enthusiasm, and indeed they have become the source of increased unity.

What causes such varied outcomes in such similar situations? Some people are willing to admit their mistakes and others are not. As a Church, and as local faith communities, we must always be willing to face our shortcomings with humility, courage, and hope. When we admit we have big problems, people start looking for big solutions.

As Christians, as Catholics, as Church, and as citizens, we must always take time to check and adjust ourselves to the compass that guides us. To do this, we must ask ourselves soul-searching questions and courageously seek answers to those questions.

What are we celebrating? is one of those questions, because you can be certain that we are becoming whatever it is we are celebrating. We must ask this question of ourselves, of our Church, of our nation, and of our culture. And we would be wise to listen attentively to the answers, because these answers will utter prophetic truths about our future. We become what we celebrate.

If you walk into most teenagers' rooms and look around, what occupies the places of prominence? Posters of rock stars and movie stars who, for the most part, live lives unworthy of any person who acts as a role model; magazines filled with articles that subtly, and not so subtly, undermine the values of our faith; compact-discs filled with music that redefines love as something selfish and sensual; and video games that stifle the individuality and kill the creativity that define a person's unique path toward God. We become what we celebrate, and this teenager will become a cloned conglom-

erate of the people and things he or she is celebrating. When our children know more about teen
pop-idols than they do about Jesus Christ, it is
time for us to reassess the place and priority our
faith has in our lives.

What are you celebrating?

The Future of Catholicism

As we look to the future, there are a great many
challenges that face the Church. In my meetings
with Catholic leaders in the United States, Europe,
and Australia, the same issues seem to emerge con-
sistently: our churches are emptying; we lack real
contact with the youth; divorce is destroying families and dividing communities; vocations to the
priesthood and religious life are scarce; and the
Church is facing a growing marginalization in the
wake of an ever intensifying secularity.

When these issues wander into the light, I have
noticed that people tend to become very defensive.
We perhaps don't like to think of the Church as
having problems, but we must, because problems
bring with them the hope of solutions. If we continue to turn our backs on the real issues, they
will continue to spread and grow like cancer in
the body. And if no one will admit there are some
big problems, no one will be looking for big solutions to those problems.

There are a great many people who think that
the problem with the world today is that people
don't come to church. They think the challenge is

to bring people to church. The real challenge is to bring the Church to the people. Fundamentally, that is what we are failing to do. We are failing to do as Christ did – namely, reach out and meet people where they are in their need, in their brokenness. We are failing to carry out the mission Christ entrusted to us through our apostolic lineage (cf. Matthew 28:16-20). We are failing to carry out the mission of the Church, which is to proclaim the good news of the Gospel to the people of every age.

If people do not come to church, it is not their failure, it is ours. We must ask ourselves, why are they not coming to church? People are not coming to church because we are failing to feed them and engage them. I don't mean entertain them. I mean engage them; that is, reach out to them where they are in their emptiness and show them how the Gospel can transform their lives. People know they are in pain, they know their brokenness, they know their emptiness, they know they have a spiritual hunger, but they think that going to church is irrelevant to modern living. Why do they think that? Because you and I have failed to show them the relevance of the life and teachings of Jesus Christ in the twenty-first century. As a Church, we have failed to show them how Jesus, the sacraments, and the Gospel can ease their pain, make them whole again, and bring meaning and purpose to their lives.

Certainly, we can become proud and obstinate and put our heads in the sand and say, "That's their problem." Or we can seek shallow consolation in the knowledge that, "the gates of hell will not prevail" (Matthew 16:18). It saddens me when people take this attitude because I don't think God wants you, me, or the Church just to survive. I think he wants us to thrive. Are you thriving? Or are you just surviving? Is the Church thriving? Or is the Church just surviving?

Your future, my future, and the future of the Church are all intimately related to one another. It is people like you and me who make up the Church. If the Church is not thriving, it is because you and I are not thriving.

The mission of the Church in this age is to share the gift of the Gospel with the people of this time in history. This is your mission. This is my mission. This is our mission together. We are the Church. The best way for us to fulfill this mission is to allow the values and principles of the Gospel to transform our own lives. The most effective messenger is the one who lives the message. Francis of Assisi said, "Preach the Gospel at all times, and only when necessary use words." Our culture is hungry for authentic lives. Let your life speak.

The Solution

In every age, the Church experiences problems and difficulties. Our time is no different. The solution to the problems that plague our lives and the Church is unchanging and singular. The problems are many; the solution is solitary. Personal holiness is the answer to every problem. In every situation of my life, in every problem, in every difficulty, I know that if I apply the values and principles of the Gospel to that circumstance, it will turn out for the best. It may not always turn out as I wish, but I will be a better person for having applied the Gospel to that situation. And because of that, my future will be richer.

Holiness is simply the application of the values and principles of the Gospel to the circumstances of our everyday lives - one moment at a time.

In every age, there is a small number of men and women who are prepared to turn their backs on popular culture and personal gain to embrace heroically the life Jesus outlines in the Gospels. These people fashion Catholicism into a lifestyle, they listen attentively to the voice of God in their lives, and they passionately pursue their personal adventure of salvation. As a result, they capture the attention and fascinate the imaginations of everyone who crosses their path. Paradoxically, the modern world pities these people because it believes they are missing out on something. Never feel sorry for them. These men and women are the happiest people who ever lived. They are the saints. In Part Two, we will discuss how they managed to live such awe-inspiring lives and discover how we can emulate their wisdom in our own lives. If the Church is to thrive in this modern era, it depends on men and women like these.

The Church, like so many other things in life, is not something we inherit from generations past or take over from our predecessors. The Church is on loan to us from future generations. Let us always remember that in the whole scheme of things, we have borrowed it for a very brief time.

The future of the Church is in our hands... and you can be certain, it will be what we make it.

Let the Celebration Begin

As Catholics, the one thing we do more than anything else is celebrate. Everything the Church does is centered around a celebration.

We celebrate life. We celebrate the changing seasons with the richness of the Church's calendar. We celebrate excellence by honoring the heroes of our faith as saints and patrons. We celebrate birth and re-birth with Baptism and burial. We celebrate truth, beauty, and goodness by seeking them out wherever they are to be found and honoring them in our everyday lives. We celebrate Christmas and Easter. We celebrate pilgrimage – our common journey and our own individual journeys. We celebrate salvation. We celebrate forgiveness with Reconciliation. We celebrate total dedication to the spiritual life with Holy Orders. We celebrate education. We celebrate communion with God and community with the Mass. We celebrate unity by seeking to bridge the gap. We celebrate love with Marriage. We celebrate...

The spirit of Catholicism is predominantly celebration. Celebration is the genius and the fundamental orientation of our faith.

—⁓—

At this time in history, both life and faith are being attacked with the full force of a culture racing toward self-destruction.   These are direct attacks on the essence of the human person.

I believe the best way to defend life is to celebrate life. I believe that the best way to celebrate life is to live our own lives to the fullest. To embrace life with both arms wide open, to lay our lives enthusiastically at the service of humanity, to love deeply the people who cross our paths, and above all, to embrace our God. Life should never be wasted. Not one moment, because life is precious.

I believe the best way to defend the faith is to celebrate our faith. The best way to celebrate Catholicism is to live the faith more fully with each passing day, allowing it to reach into every corner of our lives. When Catholicism is the foundation of our family life, our social life, our intellectual life, our spiritual life, our community life, and our professional life, then we will have established an integrated life – a life of integrity. That unity of life will speak more powerfully than any words can ever speak. And if just a handful of people in one place and one time will give their whole selves to seeking, discovering, embracing, and living this life, they will change the whole course of human history.

What are we celebrating as a culture? What are you celebrating? You have become the person you are because of the things you celebrate. Our culture has become what it is because of the things we celebrate.

You can celebrate anything you wish. You can celebrate life and faith. You can celebrate love and honesty, mercy and forgiveness, kindness and generosity. You can celebrate truth, beauty, goodness, and redemption. On the other hand, you can celebrate destruction and paganism. You can celebrate hatred and violence, selfishness and greed, contempt and disrespect. You can celebrate perversion, corruption, pride, and deceit. But one thing is certain, we become what we celebrate. This is the one immutable truth found in the life of every person who has ever lived. We become what we celebrate. It is true not only in the life of a person, but also in the life of a family. It is true in the life of a nation, and it is true in the life of the Church.

Let the celebration begin.

PART TWO

THE AUTHENTIC LIFE

Several years ago, my younger brother Nathan was living in Japan for a year as an exchange student. During that time, I received a letter from him with a photograph he had taken of what seemed to be the courtyard of an ancient Japanese garden. In the middle of the courtyard was an almond tree in full bloom. Nathan has always been a talented photographer, but what really captured my attention was a quotation he had written on the back of the photograph. The quotation was from the writings of Greco, the famed Greek-born Spanish painter. It read:

> "I said to the almond tree,
> 'Sister, speak to me about God,'
> and the almond tree blossomed."

Only one thing is necessary for Catholicism to flourish – authentic lives. Throughout history, wherever you find men and women genuinely striving to live the Christian life, the Church has always blossomed. If we wish to speak effectively to the modern world about God, the Christian life, and the Catholic Church, we must be thriving, blossoming, and flourishing in that life.

The best way to speak about God is to thrive in the life he calls us to live.

CHAPTER SIX

WHAT IS THE AUTHENTIC LIFE?

The authentic life begins with the simple but profound desire to play the part God has designed for us in human history. The unfathomable adventure of salvation begins when we stop asking, "What's in it for me?" and turn humbly to God in our hearts and ask, How may I serve? What work do you wish for me to do with my life? What is your will for my life?

Our modern times have revolted violently against the idea of "God's will." Desperate to maintain the illusion of being in control of their lives, many modern Christians have either turned their backs on God, or created a new spiritual rhetoric that allows them to determine selectively God's will for their lives. And yet, it is the very surrendering of our own will to God's designs that characterizes the whole Christian struggle. The interior life is primarily concerned with this single dynamic of turning our individual will over to God.

God calls each of us to live an authentic life. He has designed this life to perfectly integrate our legitimate needs, our deepest desires, and our unique talents. The more intimately and harmoniously these three are related, the more you become truly yourself.

God doesn't call you to live an authentic life so he can stifle or control you. He calls you to live an authentic life so that, from an infinite number of possibilities, you can become the-best-version-of-yourself. By calling you to live an authentic life, God is saying, "Be all you can be."

Fostering the Inner Life

While we are each called to live an authentic life, the exterior qualities of this life can take many different forms and tend to differ substantially from one person to the next. Some people are called to live an authentic life as husband and wife, truly committed to love in marriage. Others are called as priests and religious, dedicated to exploring the deep wells of Christian spirituality and sharing the fruits of their efforts with the community. Others still, are called to live as single persons, and use the versatility of their state in life to live and proclaim the Good News in ways that would be impossible for the married and ordained.

Professionally, some of us may work as doctors and lawyers, teachers and nurses, mechanics, bakers, and carpenters. Others may keep the home and dedicate the professional aspect of their lives to motherhood. Some may dedicate their professional energies to full-time ministry, which could include anything from counseling to volunteering at a local soup kitchen. These are all just different manifestations of the authentic life. Every honest human activity is compatible with the authentic life.

The external activity is less important than the internal transformation this activity is designed to achieve in our lives.

A man's work may be to sweep the street, but if he does it well, and hour by hour turns to God in his heart and says, "Father, I offer you this hour of work as a prayer for my neighbor Karen, who is struggling with cancer," then he has truly discovered and lived the words "pray constantly" (1 Thessalonians 5:17). He has transformed an hour of work into an hour of prayer, and his work has improved his intimacy with God and his neighbor.

This is the very essence of the inner life – the transformation of ordinary activities into prayer. Every activity of our day can lead us to experience God. Those who foster this interior life live uncommon lives in the midst of common circumstances.

The authentic life is compatible with any honest human activity.

Every honest work can be transformed into prayer. How can you transform your work into prayer? Offer the actions of your life to God as a prayer - whether it is washing the dishes, repairing a car, or studying for an exam - and by your inner intention, you will transform ordinary daily activity into the noblest task. By doing so, you will elevate tedious tasks into spiritual exercises that draw you nearer to God. This is how modern man must seek intimacy with God.

The role of work in the Journey of the Soul is, in the first place, to provide an opportunity to grow in virtue, and in the second place, to provide for our temporal needs. When our primary focus is on providing for our temporal needs and those of our family, we lose sight of the great value of work, and consequently, work becomes less of a joy and more of a drudgery.

Whether our work in this life is to be a street cleaner or a senator, we must remember that the interior effect that the work we do has on our soul is infinitely more important than the exterior fruits of our work.

Modern Despair

Toward the beginning of his reflections at Walden Pond, Henry David Thoreau observed, "Most men lead lives of quiet desperation." These words were penned and published more than one hundred and thirty years ago, and yet, they are words for our modern times. Ask yourself, is the quiet desperation Thoreau speaks of still alive in our society today? Is it present in our own lives?

Did you know that the number of people using prescribed medications for the treatment of depression is ten times greater today than it was ten years ago? Did you know that, since 1950, the suicide rate among teenagers and young adults has increased by five thousand percent? Are these just medical situations? Or should we ask ourselves and our culture what is causing this great modern despair?

As I travel the world, it is impossible not to notice how people's lives are becoming faster and busier everyday. Caught up in the day-to-day drudgery of life, smothered by the hustle and bustle, many people are tormented by the feeling that their lives are moving so fast that they just get more behind everyday. In this modern schema, most people are not thriving, they are merely surviving. And, isn't that a life of quiet desperation?

Our Essential Purpose

When we separate the daily activities of our lives from our essential purpose, it is only a matter of time before despair and desperation take a hold of us. And yet, the greatest casualty in this modern culture has been exactly that - our essential purpose.

What are we here for? What is the meaning and purpose of life? What is our essential purpose?

If you can distract a person from her essential purpose for long enough, she will become miserable. If you can prevent a whole generation from even discovering their essential purpose, you will create an epidemic of misery and despair.

The greatest tragedy of modern Catholicism is the dilution and destruction of the goal of the Christian life. My experience has been that the great majority of Catholics do not know the goal of the Christian life. Others have cast the ideal aside, saying it is not conducive to modern living. Tragically, a great many have never heard it clearly articulated.

Although I am too young to know from first-hand experience, it seems to me that after The Second Vatican Council, and perhaps before, a great many educators and priests stopped teaching, preaching, and speaking about this goal. It seems they felt it was "an unattainable ideal" or "an unrealistic goal" in the changing context of the modern world. They thought it made people feel guilty. It seems they wanted to make it easier for people. So they threw it away or watered it down.

They didn't make it easier for people; they made it harder for them. Have you ever tried to find your way to a place you have never been before with no directions, no map, and no clear description of the destination?

If you take away the goal of the Christian life, you don't make it easier for people – you make it harder. You don't bring them happiness; you start them along the road toward hopelessness and misery. People excel, thrive, and are ultimately happy when they have a higher standard to look to and strive for. I have never encountered a situation where having a goal didn't flood my spirit with hope, fill my mind with determination, and generally bring the best out of me. It is true that our goals need to be achievable. But we make the great goals of our lives achievable by breaking them down into manageable portions, while at the same time keeping the ultimate end in mind.

Our times are plagued by a great deal of confusion regarding religious thought. This confusion exists both inside and outside the Church. The prophet Amos spoke of a *famine of truth* (cf. Amos 8:11). I believe his prophecy has its time in our own day and age. The loss of "our essential purpose" is the cause of "the great modern madness."

The authentic life is a lifestyle that orients us toward the goal of the Christian life. We are called to holiness, every man and every woman without exception – regardless of our age, color, socioeconomic background, or state in life. Holiness is the goal of the Christian life and our essential purpose.

Modern man has simply become disoriented. We have lost our way. By putting aside the goal of the Christian life – this call to holiness – we have lost sight of the great Spiritual North Star. The North Star is the only star in the sky that never moves; it remains constant, unwavering, and therefore is truly a guide. If we are to find our way, we must rediscover this great Spiritual North Star.

What is Holiness?

The great confusion that is torturing the Church and weakening our faith surrounds one question. What is holiness? The falling attendance at church, the marginalization of the Church by our secular culture, and our failure to reach the youth are all caused by our inability to communicate clearly the answer to this question. What is holiness?

There are a lot of good people out there who want to know the truth and live the truth. They want to embrace God and live good Christian lives; they just don't know how to practically apply the principles of the Gospel to their everyday lives. The good people of every age cry out to their spiritual leaders, teachers, prophets, and priests, asking, "What is holiness and how do I live it in my everyday life?" They may not articulate the question in this exact form, but in essence all their questioning resolves itself if this question can be answered. If we can communicate powerfully and effectively what holiness is, and how it is practically attained, people will walk that path.

What is your view of holiness? We all have different ideas of who God is, and we all have different ideas of what it means to be holy. In your mind, does someone have to be a priest in a monastery or a nun in a convent to be holy? Do people need to be materially poor to be holy? How do you feel if you see a priest driving a nice car? What do you think? Can wealthy people be holy? Can married people be holy? Is it possible to have sexual relations and be holy? Do you view the sexual intimacy of marriage as a barrier to holiness? Do you think of sexuality as something unholy? Can you be holy? Or, do you consider holiness to be only for an elite group?

We all have a vision of what it means to be holy, and often, our vision is distorted by prejudice or tainted by ignorance. God calls each and every one of us to holiness – without exception. God calls you to holiness; he calls you to be all you can be.

Holiness is compatible with every state in life. Married people can be holy, and they are called to holiness as much as monks and nuns. Sexual intimacy is a profound gift from God, and it is an instrument of holiness. The riches of this world have value only inasmuch as they help us fulfill our essential purpose. If we own them, they can be powerful tools that can help us achieve our essential purpose. If they own us, they will prevent us from becoming all we can be. The rich can be holy, inasmuch as they use their wealth in productive ways that foster their own growth and the growth of others.

History is full of examples of men and women who have become all they were created to be – we call them saints. Some of them were priests and monks, others were nuns, some were married and others were single, some were rich and others were poor. Holiness is for everyone – no exceptions. Holiness is for you. Be all you can be.

Many people believe that if you want to be holy, you are not allowed to enjoy life. Some believe to be holy you have to run away from the world. Others think to be holy you have to be in church on your knees praying all day. Others still, believe to be holy you have to walk around with a halo – you're not allowed to smile, or have any fun, or enjoy yourself at all. They think to be holy you have to despise everything of this world and walk around with a long, drawn-out, stoic look on your face.

These are all the very unnatural and unattractive ideas that the world proclaims about holiness. The world ridicules holiness. The world pities the saints, saying, "Oh, he could have been so much more!" or "She had so much potential!" Let me assure you, it is not the saints who need pitying.

Holiness brings us to life. Holiness refines every human ability. Holiness doesn't dampen our emotions, it elevates our emotions. Those who possess holiness are the most joy-filled people in history. They have a richer, more abundant experience of life, and they love more deeply than most people can even imagine. They enjoy life, all of life. Even in the midst of suffering, they are able to maintain a peace and a happiness which is independent of the happenings and circumstances surrounding them. Holiness doesn't stifle us, it sets us free.

The surest signs of holiness are not how often a person goes to church, or how many hours a person spends in prayer, or what good spiritual books a person has read, or even the number of good works a person performs. The surest signs of holiness are an insatiable desire to improve oneself and an unquenchable concern for unholy people.

Holiness is to allow each moment to be all it can be. Holiness is to live with the goal in mind. It is to allow our decisions to be guided by the great Spiritual North Star. It is to grasp each moment and make it all it can be. Each event in your life is an opportunity to change, to grow, and to become the-best-version-of-yourself – and that grasping of each moment is holiness.

Holiness is as simple as knowing when to say "yes" and when to say "no," but like so many things in this life, we complicate the pursuit of holiness unnecessarily.

In one moment you can become holy. In any moment that you choose to be all you can be – you are holy. Any moment that you grasp as an opportunity to exercise virtue – is a holy moment. But as quickly as this holiness can be found, it can be lost, because in any moment that you choose to be less than the-best-version-of-yourself, you become unholy.

This is what it means to be striving for holiness, to be continually grasping the circumstances we call "moments" and using them to change and grow, and allowing God to transform us into all he has created us to be. And when you see it in a person, even for a moment, it is inspiring.

The truth is, virtue is ultimately attractive. When Jesus walked the earth, people wanted to be with him. Whether he was speaking in the synagogue, walking down the street, or eating at someone's home - people wanted to be with him. They crowded around him. Hung on his every word. Grasped just to touch his cloak.

There is nothing more attractive than holiness.

We know it not only in Jesus, but we know it here and now in our own day and age. When a young law clerk refuses to lie to win a case and advance her career, aren't you inspired? When you meet a man who is simple, humble, and hardworking, who immigrated from a foreign country, couldn't even speak English, but goes to work everyday to feed and educate his children, aren't you inspired? When you hear of those who labor tirelessly to feed and clothe the homeless, don't you wonder how they do it? When you meet a young woman who has rejected the culture of casual sex to save herself for her husband, aren't you moved? When you hear that the doctors and nurses at a local hospital are coaching the inner-city baseball teams, doesn't it fill you with hope?

Not only is holiness attractive, but it is inspiring.

The-Best-Version-of-Yourself

To live an authentic life is to become fully yourself. To be holy is to become fully the person God created you to be. The authentic life, the pursuit of holiness, and our essential purpose are one and the same.

More than a thousand years ago, Athanasius wrote, "The glory of God is the perfection of the creature." We do not give glory to God by presenting ourselves at Mass on Sunday, sitting in the back, paying no attention, and believing that we will have our names ticked off in some divine attendance book that exists only in our minds. We do not give glory to God by falling before his altar helplessly and hopelessly to beg him to make right what we have set wrong, or what he has given us the power to make right. Nor do we give God glory by masking our rejection of his gentle but ever present call with the occasional good deed, mindless prayer, or charitable contribution.

The glory of God is the perfection of the creature. The human person is perfected through the disciplined attainment of virtue assisted by the grace of God. The latter is never lacking; the former is the secret to a richer and more abundant future for humanity. This disciplined striving for virtue is the authentic life.

It is important to understand that the perfection that God calls us to is not some type of robotic perfection. If you asked a kindergarten class to draw and color a perfect tree, they would use hard, straight lines and bright colors. No such tree exists. But there are lots of perfect trees. Their crookedness is part of their perfection. Your big ears and your bent nose are a part of your perfection, but the defects in your character must be worked on.

In his letter to the Thessalonians, St. Paul writes, "This is the will of God: that you be saints" (1 Thessalonians 4:3). Your holiness is the desire of God, the delight of God, and the source of your happiness – to become who you were created to be, to become the-best-version-of-yourself.

Therefore, holiness is for everyone, not just for a select few. Holiness is not just for monks in monasteries and nuns in convents; it is for you and me. Our daily tasks have spiritual value. You don't work for eight dollars an hour, you work to transform your soul, to become more fully yourself, and thus, to give glory to God.

Vatican II

Ever since Vatican II, it seems we have been searching for "new" ways, "modern" ways, to reach people with the Gospel, so that they might live richer, fuller lives. On some levels we have succeeded, but on a great many others we have done little more than provide another form of entertainment.

At this time, I think it is safe to say that Vatican II was grossly misunderstood by Catholics at large and misrepresented by a great many theologians. As I read and re-read the documents, I find the overwhelming theme is not something new, but a reminder that we are all called to holiness. The documents of Vatican II are a life-based teaching that respect the classical sources and the richness of our Catholic tradition, while at the same time giving contemporary expression to these treasures. These teachings provide a worldview that is nothing short of awe-inspiring to anyone interested in seeking answers to some of the questions that face the Church and humanity at this time in history.

If you have never read the documents of Vatican II, I would like to encourage you to. Begin with *Guadium et Spes – The Church in the Modern World*. It is the last of the sixteen documents and by far my favorite. Read it slowly, reflectively, prayerfully. Take it to your time of prayer each day for a couple of weeks. Read one paragraph at a time, and from each paragraph, pick out a phrase, an idea, or a single word that jumps out at you. Use that as the beginning of a conversation with Christ. Speak to him in a gentle, mental dialogue about what you have read and how it touches you, inspires you, upsets you, or offends you. Be honest with God. If you disagree, disagree. Speak to him about why you disagree. But always remain open to the Spirit of Truth. If you don't understand something, don't let it trouble you, just move on to the next paragraph.

If we take time to read the writings of Vatican II, we will discover that the thrust of the Council's teachings was to remind us all, regardless of our age or vocation, that we are called to seek and live an authentic life – we are called to holiness. The Council sought to point out and remind us of this great Spiritual North Star. The Cardinals and Bishops who participated in the Council knew all too well that the only way Catholicism would thrive in the modern world was if we kept sight of our essential purpose.

I pray everyday that I live to see Vatican II truly implemented in the Catholic Church.

The Depression

The depression of our age is not economic, it is spiritual. There seems to be an all-pervading sense of purposelessness in many people's lives today. Why are we here? is a question many people have stopped asking and started avoiding. They have stopped asking this question not because they don't want to know the answer. They have stopped asking this question because they have seen nothing to believe that anyone has the answer, because those who have the answer have hidden it under a bushel (cf. Matthew 5:14). Remember, the human heart is on a quest for happiness, and to believe that we can find happiness without discovering our essential purpose is foolishness.

When the practice and preaching of Christianity are not clearly focused on "the universal call to holiness," the activities pursued in the name of Christianity disintegrate into nothing but a collection of social welfare initiatives. As the Church becomes more and more isolated from this call to holiness - whether locally, regionally, nationally, or universally – it very quickly begins to resemble little more than a massive social welfare committee, rather than the great spiritual entity she was established to be for every age.

There is a great need to re-identify "the essential purpose" of the human being. Whatever brave men and women will step forth and walk toward the great Spiritual North Star will do a service not only to Catholics, but also to people of every belief, because the search for meaning in our lives is universal. The Church desperately awaits a few brave souls who will stand up and remind us of our great spiritual heritage by redirecting us toward the goal of the Christian life.

We know all too well from our experiences in other areas of life - whether it is business, science, or sport – without clearly defined goals, little is achieved and most people grossly underachieve. Michelangelo once wrote, "The greater danger for most of us is not that our aim is too high and we miss it, but that it is too low and we reach it."

I believe there is a direct relationship between happiness and holiness. This was my first serious observation of the Christian life as a teenager. I must also confess, it was the reason I first began to explore Catholicism seriously. As simple as it may sound, I was aware of my yearning for happiness. I had tried to satisfy this yearning in other ways and had been left wanting. I had witnessed a peace and purpose in the lives of a handful of people I knew who were striving to live their faith, and I knew they had something I was yearning for.

My experience of people and life continually teaches me that those who have no central purpose in their lives fall easy prey to petty worries, fears, troubles, and self-pity. I have also learned that those living authentic lives are not looking over some hill or around the next corner to some elusive "future happiness." They simply try to be all they can be, and that brings with it a happiness all of its own.

God calls each of us to holiness. He calls us to be truly ourselves. This call to holiness is in response to our deep desire for happiness. We cry out to God, asking, "Show us how to find the happiness our hearts are hungry for," and God replies, "Be all you can be." It is only a logical conclusion that we will never find happiness if we are not ourselves. Imagine if a bird tried to be a fish, or if a tree tried to be a cloud. The challenge life presents to each of us is to be all we were created to be, to become truly ourselves. Not the *self* we have imagined or fantasized about, not the *self* that our friends want us to be, but the *self* God has ordained us to be from before we were in our mother's womb.

The authentic life manifests itself differently in every person. Get in touch with your essential purpose, and once you have found it, keep it always in your sight. This is the great spiritual secret of life.

CHAPTER SEVEN

THE PATH IS WELL TRODDEN

I spent much of my childhood on the sporting field in the pursuit of excellence. My seven brothers and I were constantly engaged in a variety of sporting endeavors. Each day when school was done, we went to training. Tennis, cricket, soccer, swimming, basketball, volleyball, golf, cycling, track, football... you name it. On the afternoons when we didn't have training, we would test each other's skills in the backyard of our family home in suburban Sydney.

My father always encouraged my brothers and me to watch the champions of each sport we played. Every good coach I have ever trained under, regardless of the sport, has always encouraged me to do the same. My father and my coaches wanted me to study these great athletes for two reasons: firstly, to be inspired, and secondly, to learn the techniques from the masters.

At the time, I thought I was just being trained to be competitive in the sporting arena. Little did I know how important these lessons would become in the arena of life.

Growing up, I went to church every Sunday, but I didn't begin to take an active interest in my faith until I was about eighteen. When I began to investigate the riches of Catholicism, I came to understand that God calls each of us to live an authentic life – a life of honesty and integrity. I discovered that when we pursue what is good, true, beautiful, and noble, with honesty and integrity, we are holy.

Being young and idealistic, I was immediately attracted to the ideal of holiness. The discovery of this ideal was the single most important event of my life. It was not just the discovery of an idea. It was an awakening. It was the revelation of my essential purpose. It was an eclipse that brought focus and clarity to my life. By the grace of God, and with the direction that mysteriously emerges from the Scriptures and the sacraments, in the months and years that followed, a transformation slowly began to take place in me.

Today, I am still very much in the midst of that transformation. At times it seems as if I am progressing, while at other times, I cannot help but feel that I am slipping back down a mountain I have struggled so hard to climb. All in all, I have learned that my feelings are poor indications of the work God is actually doing in my soul. I have come to believe that at every turn in the road, God is drawing us along the path whether we are aware of it or not. My courage to accept the present and my hope to look toward the future come from remembering how God has used the circumstances of my past to achieve his purpose in my life.

In Search of Excellence

Over the ten years since my original conversion experience, I have learned to apply the wisdom my coaches shared with me in the sporting realm to my pursuit of excellence in the spiritual realm. Our faith is rich with examples of great men and women who have trained tirelessly and perfected the art of firmly establishing virtue in their lives.

If you came to me and told me that you wanted to become a great basketball player, I would tell you to study the great players that have gone before you. Learn everything you can about Michael Jordan, Larry Bird, and Magic Johnson. Similarly, if you came to me and told me you wanted to be a great golfer, I would tell you to study Arnold Palmer, Ben Hogan, Jack Nicklaus, Tiger Woods, and that carefree swing of Fred Couples. Read books, watch videos, research their training techniques; find out what qualities led them to become extraordinary athletes. If you want to be a great violinist, study other great violinists. If you want to be a great artist, study other great artists. If you want to be a great business leader, study other great business leaders. And of course, this same principle applies to those of us who want to become great Catholics.

Who will you study?

There is a path that leads to the authentic life. It is not a secret path. The path to holiness is well worn.

For two thousand years men and women of all ages, from all walks of life and every social class, have been walking this path. If you came to me and told me you were going on a journey to a place you had never been before, I would advise you to travel with a guide. If you had to choose a guide, you wouldn't choose someone who had never been to where you wanted to go. You would choose an expert, someone who has made the journey before.

The spiritual life is a long and difficult journey, and we are all pilgrims on this path. There are many men and women who have gone before us who are willing to serve as our guides as we try to make this journey. Their stories provide a living legacy of spiritual wisdom. If we seek their counsel in the wisdom of their life stories, we discover that they have faced and conquered many of the snares and pitfalls that seek to trip us up along the way. If we open our hearts to their stories, we will learn from their successes and failures, and they will teach us and inspire us to become all we can be.

The Saints

Living in the midst of this modern culture, the sweet deceit of Secular Humanism calls to us with an ever increasing frequency and intensity. How can you and I muster the strength to resist the diabolical distraction of this call? The answer I am certain is no secret. The path we want to walk, the path our age desperately needs someone to explore, has been walked before. It may be covered with grass and leaves, some shrubs may have even worked their way across it, but all the same the path is there. The path of true Christian spirituality has been well worn throughout the centuries. It may be sorely neglected of late, but, for those who seek it with a sincere heart, it will not take much to rediscover... and the rewards will be infinite.

If we sincerely wish to follow Jesus, we must ask, who have been his greatest followers? Who has thrived by following Jesus? We must ask ourselves, who has walked this path before? Who has made this perilous and difficult journey? Who has embraced the adventure of salvation? And, are they available to guide us along the path today?

The answer of course is the saints. But they have become unpopular among modern progressive Catholics. We have stopped reading their stories to our children. We have taken their statues from our churches. And we have stopped reading the books they wrote.

As Catholics, we must ask ourselves an important question in relation to these spiritual ancestors of ours. Why has modern Catholicism turned its back on these great spiritual leaders?

We would be fools to believe all this has happened in response to a handful of abuses and exaggerations that have at times found their way into our relationships with the saints.

Common Objections

It is true that from time to time, some people have placed too much emphasis on the role the saints play in Catholic spirituality. It is also not uncommon for biographers of these holy men and women to portray them as if they were born saints. Many books about the lives of the saints completely ignore their struggles to overcome sinful tendencies and the great inner conflicts they experienced. Consequently, many biographies of these extraordinary spiritual champions end up reading like religious fairly tales. I suspect the authors thought they were doing the saints a favor by telling their stories without blemish. In fact, what they were doing was robbing the Church of a great treasure, namely, the wisdom these saints came by in their struggles to overcome their faults, failings, flaws, and defects. As well as this distortion of the saints, and maybe because of it, it is also true that the way some people approach the saints borders on superstition at times.

These and other similarly petty cases are what many modern Catholics cite as the reasons for their new lack of interest in the saints. I agree that these abuses should be discouraged, but the solution to the distortion or overemphasis of a good is never to abolish the good in question. Such a response only gives birth to Protestantism.

The saints have made the journey we are called to explore for ourselves. They serve as extraordinary examples of the Christian life; and after Christ, they are the best role models, guides, mentors, and coaches for those who truly desire to draw nearer to God and work out their salvation (cf. Philippians 2:12).

Some may object, saying that Christ is the only role model necessary. But the saints are living and practical proof that Christ's philosophy works. The saints show us that it is possible for a human person to be fully transformed in Christ. These rare men and women who emerge from time to time in Catholic history are proof that Jesus really has redeemed the world, and that he has sent his Spirit to empower us to make this great journey of transformation.

The truth is, the saints have lost their popularity in this modern era not because a handful of grandmothers prayed too much to St. Anthony or St. Joseph and neglected Jesus. The saints have fallen from good grace amongst modern Catholics and lost their popularity because the Church has been infected by common secular philosophy.

As we discussed in Chapter Two, the prevailing philosophies at this time in the world are Individualism, Hedonism, and Minimalism. Sadly, these philosophies have also worked their way into the lives of many Catholics, and as Catholics we have carried these philosophies like a disease into the Church. It is therefore not uncommon for modern Catholics to judge Mass on Sunday, the Church, and Catholicism by what they get out of it. This attitude is the fruit of Individualism. Similarly, most modern Catholics have abandoned almost every Catholic tradition that is not self-gratifying or requires any display of discipline. This attitude is the fruit of Hedonism. It is also very common for people to think, "I go to Church on Sunday, and I always say grace before meals. Isn't that enough?" This attitude is of course the fruit of Minimalism. Consciously or sub-consciously, we are often asking ourselves, "What is the least I can do and still be Catholic?" and "What is the least I can do and still get to Heaven?"

So, we shouldn't be surprised that many modern Catholics are uncomfortable with the saints. I suspect they are just as uncomfortable with Jesus. The real Jesus that is, not the Jesus that they have conjured up in their minds. The saints remind us of Christ's call to break with "the spirit of the world" and challenge us to reject the glamour and allure of sin and selfishness.

This break with "the spirit of the world" is real and difficult, but it is achievable. The saints are proof of that. They are also proof of the peace and joy that are born from this bold rejection of "the spirit of the world." But as modern Catholics, many of us seem content to attend Mass on Sunday, send our children to Catholic schools, and worship the gods of materialism and secularism for the other 167 hours of the week.

As Catholics, we must once again agree that the saints have a valuable contribution to make to all those who wish to live in harmony with God. Regardless of the abuses and exaggerations that have taken place in the past, we must find a genuine place in our spiritual lives for these heroes and champions of Christianity.

The Pedestal Syndrome

Much of the misunderstanding that surrounds the role of the saints in Christian spirituality is caused by our tendency to place them high on pedestals. We tell ourselves that they are different. Consciously or sub-consciously, we subscribe to the myth that God has favorites, and that the saints are God's favored few. Most of all, we convince ourselves that we are not like them.

This pedestal syndrome is not new. Men and women of every age place their heroes high on pedestals and tell themselves that these heroes are different - the elite, the favored, the chosen. Why do we do this? We place them high on pedestals, far out of our reach, so that we don't have to strive to become like them.

When Jesus was walking the earth, he encountered the very same problem. Whenever he did something extraordinary, the people of that village wanted to put him up on a pedestal and make him a king. At those moments, he always left the town or region he was in. Why? Because Jesus didn't want people to fall down helplessly before him and worship him. He was of course worthy of worship, but he wanted the highest form of worship. Jesus wanted people to imitate him. He came to show us the way. Jesus didn't come to solve all our problems. He came to show us that if we cooperate with God and with each other, we can become vessels of light and love.

If Jesus experienced this difficulty, this pedestal syndrome, as I like to call it, we shouldn't be surprised that those who have been fully transformed in Christ experience a similar problem.

The great danger is that veneration replaces imitation. When this happens, our devotion to the saints becomes hollow and borders on superstition. The temptation is simply to respect the saints from a distance, instead of following their example, studying the wisdom of their lives, and applying their lessons to our own lives.

The Rejection of Discipline

The philosophy of Christ is based on discipline, and it is discipline that our modern culture abhors and has rejected and with all its strength. It is true that Jesus came to comfort the afflicted, but as Dorothy Day pointed out, he also came to afflict the comfortable. The saints make many modern Catholics uncomfortable because they challenge us to throw off "the spirit of the world" and to embrace "the spirit of God."

Contrary to popular opinion, discipline doesn't stifle or restrict the human person. Discipline isn't something invented by the Church to control or manipulate the masses, nor is it the tool that unjust tyrants and dictators use to make people do things they don't want to do. All these are the lies of a culture completely absorbed in a philosophy of instant gratification.

Discipline is the faithful friend who will introduce you to your true self. Discipline is the worthy protector who will defend you from your lesser self. And discipline is the extraordinary mentor who will challenge you to become the-best-version-of-yourself and all God created you to be.

As loyal and as life-giving as discipline may be, its presence in the lives of modern people is dwindling. And, whether they are aware of it or not, the people are becoming spiritually ill without it.

It may be of interest to you to know how we are passing this disease on to our children. In my travels, I have noticed that one element of our lifestyles that is propelling the modern madness is the number of activities that children are involved in today. Mothers have become taxi drivers. They go from school to tennis, to soccer, to ballet, to football, to piano lessons, to basket-ball, to the drive-through at McDonald's, to choir, to baseball... and so on... and so on... and so on.

Perhaps it is time we stopped and asked ourselves, Why do our children participate in these activities? Are they just another form of entertainment? Are they just a measure of a child's social status? Or, are they directed toward some meaningful contribution in the development and education of our children?

I propose that if these activities are to have any real value in the education and development of a child, it will be because a child learns the art of discipline through these activities. And I assure you, our children will never learn the art of discipline while they are switching from one activity to another with great regu-larity. The overwhelming number of activities our chil-dren are engaged in is serving only to distract them from acquiring any real discipline in their lives, and as a result they are being firmly grounded in the superfi-ciality that is ruling our age.

The purpose of education and extracurricular activ-ities is to provide opportunities for our children to develop discipline. Once discipline is learned, it can be applied to any area of life. Those who develop this discipline go off in search of excellence and live rich-er, more abundant lives. Those who do not find this grounding in discipline do many things, but none well.

God has placed you here for some purpose, but without discipline, you will never discover that pur-pose. Without discipline, you will march slowly and surely to join Thoreau's masses living "lives of quiet desperation."

Mozart was a great composer, but did he begin as a great composer? No. He began as a great student, mastering the discipline of playing the harpsichord. Only then, from this mastery and discipline, does the individual style and genius emerge.

Did Picasso find his unique style on his first day at art school? No. First Picasso learned to paint a bowl of fruit perfectly like a photograph. Only then, having mastered the discipline of painting, did the individual style and genius that we know today as Picasso emerge.

First discipline, then genius.

In the absence of discipline, man must content himself with superficialities. This is the spell that secularism has cast on modern man. Superficiality is the curse of the modern age.

Without discipline, we are confined to soulless living and must content ourselves with work, food, momentary worldly pleasures, and anything that can help distract us from the misery of purposeless living. Without discipline, the soul dies. Slowly perhaps, but surely.

The saints' lives were firmly grounded in discipline. Our culture rejects the saints for the same reason it rejects Jesus, because they remind us of the indispensable role discipline plays in the development of the human person.

Keeping the Goal in Sight

The goal of the Christian life is holiness. Those who have attained this goal we call saints. They have found their essential purpose, they have pursued their essen-

tial purpose, they have celebrated their essential purpose. The saints followed the great Spiritual North
Star, they have quietly chiseled away at the defects and
weaknesses in their characters, they have become the-
best-version-of-themselves. They have truly applied
themselves to the Christian life. They have brought the
Gospel to life, and they have lived authentic lives. I ask
you, Who has lived more fully than the saints?

Be careful who you allow to criticize these great
men and women.

As we have already discussed, modern Catholicism
has rejected "the call to holiness." The pursuit of holiness is our essential purpose; it is the core theme of the
Gospel, the primary idea Vatican II sought to remind us
of, and the only answer to the unquenchable yearning
for happiness that preoccupies our hearts.

A statue of a saint is a physical manifestation of a
spiritual reality. We have taken them from our churches and from our homes because we don't want to be
reminded of this great call to holiness. And above
everything else, when all is said and done, the saints
challenge us to grow holy. Our discomfort with the
saints is proof of our discomfort with our calling to live
authentic lives. We have banished the saints from our
modern practice of Catholicism because, when they are
present, it is impossible to forget that we are all called
to holiness.

If we, as Catholics, were genuinely striving to become
holy, the saints and our devotion to the saints would
never suffer the criticisms and blows that are endless-

ly hurled at them today. When veneration replaces imitation, the saints lose their genuine role in Christian
spirituality.

The challenge is for you and me to open our hearts
to the call of the Gospel, which is ultimately a call to
holiness. If you open the ears of your soul and listen to
God's gentle calling, you will discover that just like the
saints you are called to holiness.

The Church has been carried throughout the ages by
the personal holiness of a handful of her members in
each place and each time. If there is to be "a new
springtime," as John Paul II has prophesied, it will be
because we rediscover this indispensable principle of
Christian spirituality. The great Spiritual North Star
hangs in the sky, calling each of us to become the-best-
version-of-ourselves.

CHAPTER EIGHT

EVEN A BLIND MAN KNOWS...

People ask me everyday, What sort of books do you read? Who inspires you? Who are your heroes and role models? Most people are then surprised to hear that I don't read that much. I love to read, but I am in fact, a very slow reader, and I read not for entertainment, but to better myself and change my life. And while I do not read for hours, I do read everyday, even if only for ten minutes. What do I read? I read the Gospels. These four books are the foundation upon which I hope to base my life more and more with each passing day. And so, everyday, even if only for ten minutes, I read from one of these four great spiritual touchstones. Apart from the Gospels, I am usually in the midst of a good spiritual book or a novel of some sort.

There are a great many people living and dead whom I admire. My parents did a wonderful job of raising my brothers and me. As a teenager, I worked after school at a drug store, delivering packages to old ladies. Brian Brouggy, the owner of the drug store, had an amazing mind, which fascinated me and helped me to develop some intellectual muscles that my formal schooling had clearly failed to develop in me. Over the years, he has become a good friend and has inspired me to strive to become the-best-version-of-myself. My two eldest brothers inspire me. I am always impressed by Mark's incredible ability to deal calmly with people, whether it is in a crisis situation or in helping them to see all they can be. And ever since I was child, I have always been in awe of Simon's generous spirit. I cannot count the number of teachers who have inspired me and continue to inspire me, from Mrs. Western in first grade and Miss Hume in third grade, to Mrs. Rutter, Mr. McCullugh, Mr. Croke, and Mr. Wade in high school. I still hear their voices in different moments of the day, guiding me, encouraging me, challenging me. I have had the most incredible run of great teachers throughout my life, both inside and outside the classroom. The list of everyday people who are an inspiration to me goes on and on.

Apart from these, there are my friends in history - Abraham Lincoln for his perseverance; Van Gogh and Mozart for their genius; Gandhi for his integrity and resolve; Michael Jordan for his ability to transform weaknesses into strengths; Dostoevski and Hemingway for their mastery of thought and storytelling; Thoreau for his love of leisure and reflection; Aristotle and

Plato for their love of wisdom... and again the list goes on and on.

These people inspire me, and I seek to gain wisdom from the lessons of their lives, but they are not my role models or heroes.

Jesus is my role model. He is my hero. While I learn from many people, he is the one whom I wish to imitate. After Jesus, my greatest inspiration comes from those who have imitated him successfully, particularly Francis of Assisi, Mother Teresa, John Vianney, Thomas More, and John Paul II. I do not worship these people, but I do greatly admire them for their virtue and integrity.

History is full of examples of people who have lived authentic lives. If we learn to absorb the lessons their lives exude, it is possible to grow wise in our youth, and prove wrong the saying, "You cannot put an old head on young shoulders." You can and we should. Those who are willing to learn from others' mistakes can live with the wisdom of the old from the earliest age. It is not necessary to make all the mistakes yourself. Those who refuse to study history must content themselves to make mistakes that have been made before.

There are very few people in the world who wouldn't say, "I wish I was younger and knew what I know now."

For as long as I can remember, I have observed and studied extraordinary people and tried to apply their wisdom to my own life. As a child first in the area of sport, later at business school in the areas of marketing and finance, and in more recent years in the areas of relationship, in my speaking and my writing, and ultimately in the area of spirituality.

—‑◦◦◦‑—

I would like to share with you now five stories that illustrate the wisdom and power of people who have opened their hearts to the will of God. They have lived in different places and at different times, but their lives are bound together by an inspiring commitment to follow the great Spiritual North Star, pursue their essential purpose, and become the-best-version-of-themselves.

People of all faiths have admired these men and women in every nation around the world. You may disagree with some of the things these holy men and women have said or done, but it is impossible for people of good will not to respect their desire to better themselves and leave the world a better place than they found it.

It is a strange thing, I have noticed, *even a blind man knows* when he is in the presence of a great light.

Francis of Assisi

At the dawn of the thirteenth century, the world was experiencing two very similar problems to those it faces today. Coins were being mass-produced, and, as a result, were quickly becoming the primary medium of exchange. This general introduction of money was creating a greed and materialism that had not existed except amongst the elite under the bartering system.

People had never hoarded eggs or grain or chickens, because they could not be stored for long periods of time without rotting or dying. But coins were cold, lifeless, and could be easily stored. Thus, the desire to amass wealth began to seduce the human heart more than ever before. The second problem of the day was that religion had become more of a habit and empty tradition than a genuine conviction. Sound familiar?

In 1182, a child was born in the tiny town of Assisi in the hills of Northern Italy. With his life, this child would address both the greed and the religious decay that plagued his day. His extraordinary example has never stopped inspiring us.

The boy's name was Francesco, the son of a wealthy cloth merchant. While his parents hoped the boy would go on to great things, perhaps become a mayor or an influential businessman, Francis seem to waste the first twenty-five years of his life frolicking about, indulging in parties and idle daydreams of becoming a great knight. Francis was a leader and a favorite among the young people of Assisi. The life of every party, he spent endless nights in the frivolous pursuit of wine, song, and dance. Full of charm and wit, Francis was loved by all.

At twenty years of age, Francis decided he was ready to embrace what he believed to be his chance at greatness. He left Assisi in full armor, upon the finest horse, to take part in the battle between Assisi and nearby Perugia.

During the battle, Francis was knocked from his horse and later captured by the enemy. As the son of a wealthy man, Francis was held hostage for ransom.

Only after several months was he released, and by this time he had become very ill.

His convalescence provided the necessary meeting ground for Francis to encounter God. Within this stillness and solitude, the heart of the young man began to soften and transform.

Though Francis recovered from his grave illness, he would never again be the frivolous fun-seeker the people of Assisi had come to know and love. All his glory-seeking had revealed to him a profound dissatisfaction, a restlessness lurking in his soul that would not be ignored.

While in his former life he wasted countless hours with crowds of rowdy friends, now he sought the solitude of time alone in the quiet fields that surrounded Assisi.

A turning point in his new life occurred one day, when he visited the abandoned and dilapidated church of San Damiano nearby Assisi. Entering the weary structure, he knelt before the crucifix to pray. At that moment, Francis heard a voice speak to him, saying, "Rebuild my Church. As you can see, it is in ruins."

Believing he had heard the voice of God, Francis set about rebuilding the crumbling church of San Damiano. Using materials bought with his father's money or begged from the people of Assisi, Francis fully restored the little church with his own hands. He then set about rebuilding the abandoned church of St. Peter, and finally restored the also dilapidated Portiuncula, which later became the center of life for Francis and his brothers.

Once the Portiuncula was completed, Francis again heard the voice of God saying, "Francis, rebuild my Church. As you can see, it is in ruins." On this occasion, his heart was opened to understand that the voice was not calling him to a life of physical laboring to rebuild churches. Francis was being called to a spiritual mission.

Francis then turned his back on all worldly wealth to embrace a life of simplicity, humility, poverty, and prayer.

His spirit of uncompromising commitment to the Gospel has remained a force of renewal in the Church in every place and time for more than 1000 years.

Francis of Assisi has endured as one of the most intriguing figures of human history. Today there are more than one million Franciscan friars and brothers around the world. Have you ever tried to get people to volunteer for a couple of hours? Imagine inspiring more than a million people to give their whole lives for a cause.

During his lifetime, this little man of poverty became and continues to be a worldwide influence.

He has inspired and influenced the great thinkers of every age. He is the subject of hundreds of books, thousands of studies, numerous motion pictures and documentaries, and a myriad of musical compositions honor his life. If you travel the world, you will come upon countless rivers, mountains, roads, and even cities named after Francis – the most famous is of course San Francisco.

He has been hailed by historians, praised by religious leaders of all beliefs, and quoted by presidents. He has inspired artistic masterpieces including works by Rembrandt, who was by his own admission an anti-Catholic Protestant, yet was enamoured by the life and virtue of Francis. It was Francis who invented the Créche, or Nativity scene, to draw attention to the powerful paradox of God's son being born into the poverty of a stable. Every year, millions of homes and churches honor the memory of Francis with the Nativity scenes they place in their homes. As the universal symbol for a lover of nature, Francis is the statue most commonly placed in the garden.

He was all this in the past, and I believe he remains a powerful and trustworthy spiritual guide to the people of our own troubled times.

But what I delight in most about Francis is that the people who loved him honored him by remembering his story - all of his story, even his wild youth and his moments of impatience during the early days of his ministry. It is for this reason that biographers have been so successful at portraying Francis as a "whole man," rather than as a caricature of holiness. He was certainly saintly, but not sanctimonious. He loved God, but he also loved his neighbor and creation.

Francis was real. He was striving with all his heart to live an authentic life. And like the first Christians, he captured the imaginations and intrigued the hearts and minds of people of his time and the people of times to come. Francis is a practical example of the power of one authentic life indelibly engraved upon history.

Mother Teresa

Who is Agnes Bojaxhiu? Mother Teresa was born Agnes Bojaxhiu in Serbia on August 26, 1910. Agnes grew up in Albania, surrounded by wealth and prosperity. Despite their wealth, her parents were models of virtue. They loved each other deeply, and that love overflowed to Agnes and her sister. At the age of eighteen, Agnes left home to join an Irish order. Later that year, in December of 1928, she set sail for India to begin her work as a novice for the Loreto Order.

Now Sister Teresa, she spent most of the next twenty years teaching. In 1937, she made her permanent vows of poverty, chastity, and obedience, and as was customary, she adopted the title of "Mother." By 1943, India was torn by war and famine. Mahatma Gandhi's great success in freeing India from British rule had become tainted by civil war between Muslims and Hindus living in India. More people than ever descended upon Calcutta. It finally became necessary for the Loreto Convent to move the children and the school outside the city. At this time, many nuns and whole orders decided to leave India and close their schools, but Mother Teresa stayed and worked tirelessly. As others left, she taught more and more classes, eventually teaching two subjects to eight grades.

She was happy in her work and well liked. By the mid-1940s, her mere presence already had a power that had been borne through hours of prayer and reflection. Soon Mother Teresa was appointed headmistress, and she wrote to her mother, "...This is a new life. Our center here is very fine. I am a teacher, and I love the work. I am also Head of the whole school, and everybody wishes me well." Her mother's reply was a stern reminder of her original intentions for going to India: "Dear child, Do not forget that you went to India for the sake of the poor."

Kipling described Calcutta as "the city of a dreadful night." Mother Teresa was in the capital of poverty, a poverty that most people never see in their whole lives. Have you been there? Have you seen it on television? Can you picture it?

Whole families living in the streets, along the city walls, even in places where throngs of people congregate and pass through everyday. Day and night, they live out in the open. If they are lucky, they have mats that they have made from large palm leaves – but frequently they are on the bare ground. They are virtually naked; at best, they wear ragged loincloths. And as you pass along the streets, you may chance upon a family gathered around a dead relative, wrapped in worn red rags, strewn with yellow flowers, his face painted in colored stripes. Horrifying scenes, everywhere you turn. The people are covered in sores - their ears, their feet, their legs. Here and there, you will spot a man or a woman, you cannot tell which, half-consumed by maggots and on the point of death. They have lumps and lesions on their backs. Many have tuberculosis. All need medicine, and clothes, and food, and shelter.

This was the world that surrounded the school and this was the world that was crying out for help.

In 1946, Mother Teresa became very ill herself and was ordered by doctors to have bed rest for three hours every afternoon. It was very hard for her to rest and not do her work, but this period of enforced rest culminated in the directive to go away on retreat for a month.

The intention was that, in the interests of her health, she should undergo a period of spiritual renewal and a physical break from her work.

On September 10, 1946, she boarded a train for Darjeeling where she was to retreat. Aboard that train, Mother Teresa had a supernatural experience that changed the direction of her life forever. She referred to it as "the call within the call." The retreat provided the perfect period of silence, solitude, and prayer to follow the experience God had given her on the train.

The next couple of years were filled with dialogue between her spiritual director, the Bishop, and Rome. Finally, by 1950 Mother Teresa had left the school and the Loreto Order, founded the Sisters of Charity, and was living among the poorest of the poor in Calcutta.

Over the next five decades, Mother Teresa emerged as an icon of modern holiness. Dedicated to a life of simplicity, she gave herself to society's most marginalized victims. Her love for people was tangible. You could see it. You could feel it. You could reach out and touch it. It was real and living. It wasn't a sermon or a speech. When all is said and done, she loved people. Each moment, she looked only for the next opportunity to love. For her, every individual mattered. "I believe," she once said, "in person-to-person contact. Every person is Christ for me, and since there is only one Jesus, the person I am meeting is the one person in the world at that moment." Those who spent time with her would often comment, "For the moment you were with her, there was only you and her. She wasn't looking over your shoulder to see what was happening around you. You had her full attention. It was as if nothing else existed to her except you."

Contrasted against the unbridled materialism of the modern world, Mother Teresa had an attraction that seemed impossible to explain. The contrast between "the spirit of the world" and the spirit of this woman was breathtaking. Years before, the people of India had traveled hundreds of miles, often by foot, to catch a glimpse of Gandhi. Hindus believe that simply to be in the presence of a holy person brings with it a great blessing. Now they sought the company, the mere presence, even just a glimpse of Mother Teresa. Like a magnetic field, she attracted the rich and the poor, the weak and the powerful, irrespective of race or creed.

In time, Mother Teresa was awarded the Nobel Peace Prize, the United States Medal of Freedom, and the United Nations Albert Schweitzer Prize. Considered by many to be "a living saint," she didn't allow all the attention to distract her and remained a soul wholly dedicated to a life of service.

Mother Teresa is one of the most beloved women of all time. She was a steadfast voice of love and faith, and yet, her power didn't come from the words she used or the awards she received, and she never forced her beliefs upon anyone. Asked to speak about religion, she once said, "Religion is not something that you or I can touch. Religion is the worship of God — therefore a matter of conscience. I alone must decide for myself and you for yourself, what we choose. For me, the religion I live and use to worship God is the Catholic religion. For me, this is my very life, my joy, and the greatest gift of God in his love for me. He could have given me no greater gift."

The questions I ask myself are: Where does this power to love so deeply come from? Where does the strength to serve so selflessly come from? What is the source of this woman's extraordinary ability to inspire?

Before everything else, Mother Teresa was a woman of prayer. Each day, she would spend three hours before the Blessed Sacrament in prayer. Her power to love, her strength to endure, and her gift to inspire the masses were all born in the Classroom of Silence. This woman believed in the centrality of Jesus Christ. She knew his centrality in history and eternity, and she trusted in his centrality in her own life. There lies the source – she placed Jesus at the center of her life.

In the depths of her heart, she knew that action without prayer was worth nothing.

The Curé of Ars

John Vianney was born in the sleepy town of Dardilly, France, on May 8, 1786, three years before the Storming of the Bastille. About five miles northwest of Lyons, Dardilly was home to less than one thousand people, and for much of the French Revolution remained a very peaceful place to live. But at seven years of age, John's mind was far from the troubles that plagued his homeland. The son of a farmer, each day he drove the donkey, the cows, and the sheep down the valley to graze.

It was around this time that the violence of the Revolution reached his hometown in a very subtle form. Catholicism had been outlawed. A price was on the head of every priest in France, and they fled. Church bells were silenced, and Mass could not be attended without risking one's life, even if one could find a priest brave enough to celebrate. Those who were found to be harboring priests were also in great danger. This didn't stop Matthew Vianney, John's father. Priests were very often the secret guests of the Vianneys, and on other occasions, the whole family would set out in the middle of the night to attend Mass offered by a hunted priest in a nearby barn.

John grew to admire these brave and holy men, and within that admiration grew the seed of his love for the priesthood.

In the early dawn of April 18, 1802, the bells of Notre Dame in Paris rang out and proclaimed the resurrection of Catholicism in France. Now sixteen, Vianney already had his heart set on the priesthood, but as his brother Francis had been drafted and his sister Catherine was to be married, his father desperately needed him to help with the farm and refused to give consent. But by the time John was nineteen, his mother had pleaded with his father to let him go, and finally he entered minor-seminary.

Despite his tireless efforts, John Vianney struggled in his studies, particularly with Latin. It was for his lack of knowledge in Latin that he was dismissed from major-seminary in 1813 after only two months. But Father Balley, *Curé* (which means Pastor) of the church that the Vianney family attended in nearby Escully, sent him straight back with a letter to the rector. Shortly after, Vianney was dismissed again. This time, Father Balley went to the chancery and begged with the Vicar-General on account of John's great devotion to prayer and the Church.

With much assistance and some generous overlooking of his academic weaknesses, Vianney was finally ready to be ordained, and a date was set for August 13, 1815.

Once ordained, Vianney was sent to his old friend and mentor, Father Balley in Escully. Here, the old priest shared his wisdom and experience with the young priest. But late in 1817, Father Balley died. John wept like a child at the death of this good and holy priest and later wrote of him, "I have seen some beautiful souls, but none so beautiful!" From that day on, Vianney mentioned Father Balley in his prayers at Mass everyday.

In February of 1818, John Vianney became the Curé of Ars. Ars was a tiny place twenty-two miles from Lyons with only sixty families. Most maps of France did not include it, and it was considered to be the Siberia of the diocese.

During those first weeks, Vianney spent his time visiting each of the sixty families. He would talk to them about the crops, the children, the relatives, and every aspect of life. What he was really doing was making a moral assessment of his parish. He found that the people's spiritual lives were in great need of restoration. They cared little for the Church, as they had been seduced by the pleasures common to every age: slothfulness, drunkenness, blasphemy, and impurity.

The new Curé understood the meaning and value of the words, "This kind can only be cast out by prayer and fasting" (Matthew 17:20). Father Vianney began a one-man campaign of prayer and fasting, offering all his efforts to God for the conversion of the people in his parish.

Many considered his penances too severe. He slept on the floor, went for days without food, and at one time ate nothing but a boiled potato each day for several years. But the graces borne from his sacrifices brought clarity to his mind, and they flooded his soul and the souls of his parishioners with abundant graces.

The Curé preached boldly and without reservation about the evils of his community. In the early days, he spoke out against the taverns and tavern owners who "steal the bread of poor women and children by selling wine to drunkards." One man closed his tavern at the urging of the Curé, but seven more opened within a year. Father Vianney responded, saying, "You shall see, you shall see, those who open an inn in this place shall be ruined."

The people reacted violently at first, but in time the Curé's prayer and fasting began to reap a great harvest. It may have taken twenty years, but Ars was eventually rid of all taverns. And as the taverns began to disappear, other things began to disappear also. By the 1850s, Ars was rid of destitution, and the wisdom of the Curé's ways became evident. By suppressing the taverns, he had eliminated the main cause of poverty.

But the years between his arrival in Ars and the golden years of Ars were a time filled with tremendous trials and suffering for Vianney. Letters of false accusations flooded the Bishop's office, and inquiries were made into his behavior in the small rural parish. In speaking out against the evils of the village, he pricked the consciences of many, and those consciences often became hostile. Ignorance and sin confuse us, and in our confusion we cause suffering to those who are truly holy. Late in his life, Vianney wrote, "If on my arrival in Ars, I had foreseen all that I was to suffer there, I would have died on the spot."

But the pain of his life was eased by a rare spiritual pleasure. He was seeing the transformation in the people's lives. Careless people were becoming good people; good people were growing better; and the men and women who had established the habits of virtue in their lives were practicing the heroism of saints.

For his own prayer, Father Vianney spent long periods in front of the Blessed Sacrament early in the morning and late at night. He encouraged his people to make regular visits to the church and sit before the Blessed Sacrament. The good Curé knew that the Blessed Sacrament was the most powerful means of renewing the life of the parish.

Each morning, he would sit in his confessional, hearing the confessions of any who wished to come. At about the same time each day, he would hear a loud clanging noise at the back of the church. Five or ten minutes would pass and then he would hear a loud clanging noise again. He was always curious about this noise. One morning he came out of the confessional just as the second clang was ringing out. He hurried to the back of the church and found the one of the farmers leaving the church with his tools.

The Curé asked the man, "Do you come here every morning?" "Yes, Father," he replied. "What do you do here?" the Curé inquired. "I just sit a little and pray," said the simple farmer. "How do you pray?" the good priest asked. The man was aware of his own simplicity and a little embarrassed. He bowed his head and said, "I look at the good God, and the good God looks at me."

Father John Vianney was a man of prayer and good living, and the people of his parish became people of prayer and good living. He was, first and foremost, a spiritual leader to his people, and took seriously the responsibility of guiding their souls along the path of salvation.

But his influence was not confined to the people of Ars. From his earliest days in Ars, the people from his hometown of Dardilly and the people of Escully, where he had first served as assistant, came to him for spiritual direction. On their way to and from Ars, people would ask where they were going and why, and word would spread very quickly of the "Holy Curé" as they called him.

Between 1827 and 1859, the church at Ars was never empty. At first, there were twenty visitors a day, but in time the floodgates opened, and people streamed to this sleepy little village a thousand at a time. During the last year of Father Vianney's life, more than 100,000 people came to Ars. So many people were visiting Ars that a spur had to be added to the train line. Within ten years of his death, that very same track was torn up again, as it was used so little. In the mid-1800s, Ars became the great focal point of spirituality in France. Why? Because of one simple, humble, holy priest.

Why did the people come?

People of all ages are hungry for God. Whenever a man or woman emerges as an instrument of God's truth and goodness, people will beat a path to that person's door. The reason people flocked to see the Curé of Ars is no different. In his preaching, in his advice, and in confession, they sensed the truth, goodness, and guidance of God himself.

Above everything else, the Curé of Ars was a confessor. As the crowds came to Ars, Vianney simply increased the number of hours he spent in the confessional. Sometimes he would spend twelve, fourteen, sixteen, even eighteen hours a day hearing the confessions of pilgrims. As for the pilgrims, some of them waited in line for three days to have the Curé hear their confession or to ask his advice on a matter. He served his God and his people with the sublime monotony of routine.

His words were penetrating and challenging. He spoke to his penitents with the same boldness and clarity with which he preached.

As his popularity soared, so did the criticisms of him. His colleagues, the priests of France, remembered well his lack of education. And as the people of France began to speak of him as a "living saint," great jealousy took a hold of many. But the Curé would not allow any of this to interfere with his work. The more he was exulted, the more he humbled himself.

On August 4, 1859, John Marie Vianney, the Curé of Ars, died. Many may look at John Vianney's life and say he did a great many strange things. But the motives behind these seemingly strange actions were as pure as the fallen snow. If we can resist the temptation to cast his ways off as absurd and impractical, behind all of his actions we will find a profound and deeply moving love of God and neighbor.

Vianney believed indifference toward religion and a lust for material comforts were the obstacles to true spirituality in his time. With his own life, he showed us all that there is another way.

Thomas More

Thomas More was born in London on February 7, 1478. He served as a pageboy to the Archbishop, who was so impressed that he sent Thomas to Oxford University when he was only 14 years old. During his time at Oxford, he became tutor to the prince who would later become King Henry VIII. As a young lawyer still in his 20s, More was elected to Parliament and there began his meteoric rise in the political world.

More was monumentally successful. He was respectably born, but not nobly. The son of a merchant-class family, he distinguished himself first as a scholar, then as a lawyer and judge, later as an Ambassador, and finally, in the highest and most prestigious post in England as Lord Chancellor.

Although Thomas was a man of considerable means, his lifestyle was often more akin to that of an ascetic monk. He owned multiple homes, barns, and farming lands; employed live-in servants and private tutors for his children; and collected exotic animals and artifacts as a hobby. A guest book at his estate in Chelsea would have been more like the *Who's Who* of the sixteenth century; Holbein, Erasmus, and Colet were among his noted guests. Thomas More corresponded with all the great minds of Europe and was himself considered a remarkable statesman and one of the great minds of his time. His home became known as a center of laughter, learning, and good conversation. He was a friend to the King, who often called upon More to advise him or simply to keep him company. On occasion and in unprecedented fashion, he visited More in his own home.

Thomas More adored and was adored by his own large family. He raised his children in the disciplines of education and virtue, and was himself a worthy role model in both. In a time when women were thought to be not worth educating, he provided a fine education for his daughters.

He was a celebrated writer during his own time, and his writings continue to be widely studied today. Thomas' sociopolitical fantasy *Utopia* describes his dream of an ideal society, and gave a name to a literary genre and a worldview.

Thomas More was a remarkable man. He loved life, and he celebrated life. He was admired even by those who opposed him, he was successful beyond imaginings in numerous fields, he was devoted to his family, but above all, he was a man who found the grace necessary to live with integrity when it would have been easier not to.

When Thomas More parted with his life, he parted with more than most men, and that makes his action even more powerful and meaningful.

—⁓—

In the spring of 1534, Thomas More was imprisoned in the Tower of London for refusing to sign the Act of Supremacy. Henry VIII wanted to divorce his wife, Catherine of Aragon, and marry Anne Boleyn, so he petitioned the Pope for an annulment. But, as the Pope had already granted a special dispensation for Henry to marry Catherine, his deceased brother's wife, the request was denied. Henry became furious and set his stubborn mind on marrying Anne all the more. As a

result, Henry decided to separate the Church in
England from the Church in Rome, and by an Act of
Parliament, appoint himself the Supreme Head of the
Church in England. It was this Act that Thomas More
refused to sign and support.

Thomas More was an intelligent man. He knew that,
by law, he could be imprisoned for not signing the Act,
but not put to death. The law considers silence to be
consent, but the silence of a man of virtue is louder
than most men's words. Thus, England began to buzz,
guessing at the opinions of Thomas More.

Henry didn't want to kill Thomas, and at any
moment until his execution, he was willing to pardon
More if he would simply agree to give public approval
of Henry's marriage with Anne Boleyn. The King wanted Thomas' imprimatur. He had the signatures of
dozens of leading officials and statesman on the document, but the endorsement of immoral men is not
worth having. The people of Europe paid no attention
to who had signed the Act; they were fixated on who
had not. Thomas was a man of virtue, and his character and reputation were undisputed. So naturally, the
King wanted his approval.

All this presented a problem for More. He could not
in good conscience sign the Act, because his well
informed mind and his well formed conscience told
him clearly that Parliament didn't have the authority to
appoint the King as the Supreme Head of the Church in
England. Parliament didn't have the authority because
this was a spiritual office, not a political office.

Most men would have given in and signed the Act.
Most men did. But Thomas was a man with a remarkable sense of his own "self." He was not a stubborn,

hardheaded man. He knew how to compromise in situations for his wife, his children, even his friends, but refused to compromise his "self." The greatest possession a person has is his own immortal soul – and Thomas knew this truth with unwavering clarity.

A person takes an oath only when he wants to commit himself to the statement, and not just himself but his "self" – his immortal soul. In an oath, a man gives himself as a guarantor. He stands before God and joins his "self" with the truth, or in this case the lie, of the oath. The oath of a man willing to perjure himself is not worth having, because we sense that he has no "self" to commit, no guarantee to offer, for he has given it away or sold it. This is why in the modern world we prefer people to guarantee their statements with cash, rather than with themselves.

Since I was a child, I have heard the phrase "every man has his price." Thomas teaches us that this needn't be so. Life tests us all in this department, and Thomas More was no different.

Most men and women can be bought, and bought quite cheaply. Some men and women can be bought with money, power, status, or possessions; others are bought with pleasure, land, bricks and mortar, knowledge, or fame. Men who are able to maintain possession of their "self" in the midst of these offerings are few. The world then tries to buy these rare souls with suffering. Not that you can buy a man by offering him suffering, but you can impose suffering and offer him escape from that suffering.

This is how Henry VIII, Thomas Cromwell, the Church of England, history, and "the spirit of the world" tried to purchase the soul – or "self" – of Sir

Thomas More. They threw him in prison. They tried to separate him from everyone and everything that he loved. Hoping that in that cold, dark, lonely cell deprived of food, light, and human contact, he would break and give his "self" to their will.

But, they had mistaken Thomas for themselves. They had forgotten that Thomas was a man of prayer and virtue. His "self" was non-negotiable, and had become so by the practice of temperance and long hours at prayer. In the midst of abundance, he hadn't allowed himself to get carried away, and now, in the midst of poverty, he was not disconcerted.

Thomas also proved that it is possible to be a politician and keep your character intact, despite the dishonest and self-seeking environment that surrounds you. He is one of history's most authentic models of selfless and virtuous leadership. Imagine what America would be like if we had a man of Thomas More's character and virtue as President.

Thomas More faced and overcame the enticements of this world. He was truly able to live amidst the world, and yet, not belong to the world. I pray you and I can develop the sense of self that Thomas More had.

I became fascinated with Thomas More for the first time when I worked as a stagehand for my high school's production of *A Man for All Seasons*. I was intrigued by this man who so obviously had his own life in his hands, and yet, chose to die. As the years have passed, I have become more and more in awe of him. No one could accuse him of any incapacity for life. He embraced life, fully seizing every opportunity to explore its great variety. He loved deeply and was loved deeply. He was successful and admired. Thomas

More was no plaster-cast saint; he was a man who loved life and was full of life. And yet, he found something within himself without which life was valueless. So when cruel and selfish men tried to take that "something" from him, he chose to embrace death rather than surrender it.

I hope you and I can find that something within ourselves.

John Paul II

The great men and women of history are usually born in the most unexpected places at the most unexpected times. Karol Wojtyla was born in the small provincial city of Wadowice, Poland, on May 18, 1920. Who would have known, who would have believed, that this Polish boy would become arguably the most influential figure of the twentieth century?

The life of Karol Wojtyla staggers the imagination. We all have great moments in our lives, but for one man to be so centrally involved in so many aspects of life and so many historical moments, seems almost unbelievable. If it were fiction, we would dismiss it as too far-fetched to be a valid offering.

And so, with the brief time I have to speak with you about his life, the most I can hope for is to sketch out some of his story. I do this with the hope that you will be inspired to learn more about this man we call John Paul II, and in learning more, I have no doubt you will be all the more inspired.

—*wv*—

Karol Wojtyla's mother dies before he turns ten, leaving his father, a retired military officer, to raise him. His father teaches him the art of life – discipline - and firmly grounds him in the habit of prayer. These would become the pillars of Wojtyla's life. In his youth, he is the best student in town, an enthusiastic athlete, and an amateur actor.

He later moves to Krakow with his father and enters Jagielonian University. Again, he excels in the classroom and on the stage, but his promising progress in both these areas are cut short by World War II. It is then that he forms his bond with "the worker." Working himself as a quarryman and blaster, he comes to understand the plight of the worker and the value of manual labor in man's life. In defiance of his country's Nazi occupiers, he joins a cultural resistance movement. When parish priests are kidnapped and taken to Dachau, he receives his first formal training in classic spirituality under the guidance of a lay mystic.

After the death of his father in 1941, Wojtyla begins the internal struggle of discerning his vocation. He is torn between two worlds. The altar or the stage? After considerable prayer and anguish, he sees clearly, and joins the clandestine seminary run by the Archbishop of Krakow. He continues to work at a chemical factory, while studying his philosophy and theology on the side. At night, he makes his way through the streets, risking his life, to attend classes at the Archbishop's residence.

When Poland is "liberated" by the Red Army, he is ordained a priest on November 1, 1946. He is immediately sent to Rome for graduate studies in theology. The following year, he visits France and Belgium, where he is exposed for the first time to the way of the worker-priest.

Having completed his studies in Rome, he returns to Poland and begins an intense and very personal ministry to university students. It is here that he first develops his almost unquenchable patience with dialogue and his uncanny ability to listen even to those with whom he disagrees. He forms a number of innovative workshops and seminars, engages the students in intense conversation, and spends thousands of hours in the confessional – all of which reveal a very different type of priest than the Polish people are used to. His style, which is received as a breath of fresh air, inspires the students to give him the nickname of "Wujek," which means "Uncle."

In 1954, after receiving his second doctorate, Wojtyla is invited to join the philosophy department of Catholic University of Lublin. He commutes via overnight train to his classes, and is greeted by standing room only crowds in his classes. In 1960, he raises eyebrows everywhere with his first book *Love and Responsibility*, in which he celebrates human sexuality as a gift from God for the sanctification of husband and wife.

At the age of thirty-eight, he is consecrated Bishop, and is named Auxiliary Bishop of Krakow. Between 1962 and 1965, he attends all four sessions of the Second Vatican Council. At the Council, he plays a pivotal role in designing a new Catholic openness to the modern world and raises his voice in the Council's efforts to define religious freedom and basic human rights.

After he is named Archbishop of Krakow, he begins a relentless battle for the religious and civil rights of his people. At forty-seven, he is named Cardinal, but refuses to act in the way senior prelates are expected to act. He continues to ski, hike, and kayak; he even vacations with lay people. In Krakow, he is the driving force behind the most comprehensive implementation of Vatican II. While more and more demands are made on his time, he continues to work as an intellectual – teaching, conducting seminars, writing, and delivering papers at international conferences.

On October 16, 1978, Karol Wojtyla is elected the 264th Bishop of Rome and takes the name John Paul II. The world is shocked. He is the first non-Italian Pope in 455 years and the first Slavic Pope ever.

In 1979, Pope John Paul II visits his homeland for the first time as the leader of the Roman Catholic Church. Poland comes to a standstill as millions neglect work and school to greet the man they grew to love as "Wujek." He draws the largest crowds in Polish history and single-handedly revitalizes Catholicism in a land tormented by Communism. These enormous crowds would become one of the many trademarks of his papacy. During that visit, he reawakens the conscience of Poland, and the non-violent collapse of the Soviet empire in eastern Europe begins.

John Paul II breathes new life into the world's oldest institution, the papacy, in the context of the modern world. He travels to every corner of the globe, preaching the Gospel to millions of people with each appearance. He writes and teaches endlessly, covering every aspect of Catholicism and every issue that faces humanity in the modern world. And, not to be forgotten, is the way he masterfully harnesses every modern means of communication to remind the world of the truth and light of God.

On May 13, 1981, Pope John Paul II is shot in St. Peter's Square. He survives this assassination attempt and returns to his work with more vigor than ever before. He redefines the relationship between the Catholic Church and Judaism, he asks the Orthodox Catholics and non-Catholic Christians to imagine a papacy that could serve all Christians, he preaches to Muslim teenagers in Casablanca, and describes marital intimacy as an icon of the interior life of God.

Under the weight of his relentless efforts to educate and unite Catholics, and indeed all of humanity, his health begins to deteriorate. The international press pronounces him dying, and television stations around the world commission documentaries in preparation for his departure from the world stage.

Defying all expectations in the next year, he preaches to the largest crowd ever gathered in human history on the least Christian continent of the world; he publishes a book that becomes an international bestseller and is translated into forty languages; he urges Catholics to cleanse their consciences, both individually and collectively, on the eve of the new millennium; and, he single-handedly redirects an international gathering on population issues.

In 1995, he defends the universality of human rights in his address to the United Nations. Two days later, celebrating Mass in Central Park, he both jokes with the crowd and delivers one of his characteristically challenging homilies.

Who is this man? Where does his extraordinary strength and wisdom come from?

Let me ask you, have you ever seen the Pope pray? Each morning, he celebrates Mass in his private chapel with about twenty guests. Perhaps you have been fortunate enough to attend. If not, perhaps you have seen television footage of these Masses.

When that man kneels down to pray after Communion, he closes his eyes and goes to a place deep within himself. Once he is there, nothing and no one are going to distract him from that place.

He goes to that place, deep, deep, within himself, and from that place, he brings forth the fruit of his life: wisdom, compassion, generosity, understanding, patience, courage, insight, forgiveness, humility, and a love so apparent you can almost grasp it.

The amazing thing is, if you put this same man in a football stadium with 100,000 people and a million more distractions, he will still kneel down after Communion, close his eyes, and he goes to that place deep within him. He allows nothing to distract him from his prayer.

Find that place within you.

I pray I can visit that place within me and go there more and more frequently.

Whatever name you give him, whether it be Wujek, Karol Wojtyla, Papa, John Paul II, or His Holiness - he is, first and foremost, a man of prayer. His primary concern is doing the will of God in his own life and encouraging others to do the same. To try to understand him separate from his spirituality is at best a waste of time.

He is a sign of hope and a sign of contradiction. He is priest, prophet, and pope. John Paul II is a man perfectly suited to this age, and yet, a man before his time.

It will take centuries for the collective human consciousness to understand and truly appreciate his depth, insight, and wisdom.

He carries himself in such a way that you cannot help but have ultimate respect for him, even if you disagree with his point of view. Within him, he carries a truth and a wisdom that are so evident, so apparent, that people of all religious beliefs are awed by his presence.

He is the living example of God's paradox at this moment in history. He is so old, and so weak, and so physically powerless – yet, God continues to use him as a powerful instrument of his love in the world (cf. 1 Corinthians 1:27).

At every moment of his life, from his earliest childhood, all those who encountered him were able to see his star rising. Those close to him knew his star would rise, but when, where, and in what way, nobody knew. They waited with anticipation, and having waited so patiently, none were to be disappointed.

Taking the Gospel Seriously

Francis of Assisi, Mother Teresa, John Vianney, Thomas More, and John Paul II are just five examples drawn from hundreds, no thousands, of men and women who over the past 2000 years have taken the Gospel seriously. In their lives, you can catch a glimpse of how your life will unfold if you begin to take the life and teachings of Jesus seriously.

CHAPTER NINE

WHAT SETS THEM APART?

What is it that sets those who achieve extraordinary things apart from the rest of us? Some people would tell you it is freak luck or mere chance. Others will tell you that these favored few had better connections with people of power and influence, or that they simply found themselves in the right place at the right time. It is the opinion of others still that God has favorites and that these men and women are his chosen ones.

Do not allow your hearts and minds to be deceived. There are two great differences between the heroes, leaders, champions, and saints that fill the history books, and the rest of us. In the first place, they had a singleness of purpose that penetrated every activity of their lives. And in the second place, they formed habits in their lives that helped them to achieve their goals.

Singleness of Purpose

As you study the lives of extraordinary people, you discover that their lives are all marked with these two qualities. It doesn't matter if it is Bill Gates, Michael Jordan, or Mother Teresa; these two qualities can be found in each of their lives. Bill Gates wanted to become the richest man in the world. He clearly defined his goal and thus had singleness of purpose. Then he created habits in his life that would help him achieve his goal. Michael Jordan wanted to become the greatest basketball player in history. He had a clearly defined goal and therefore singleness of purpose. Then he formed habits that enabled him to achieve his goal. The same is true of Mother Teresa and of all the saints that honor the pages of Christian history. Mother Teresa wanted to become a saint, the-best-version-of-herself. She clearly defined her goal and allowed this singleness of purpose to penetrate the everyday activities of her life.

You may object, saying, "To become the richest man in the world or the greatest basketball player in history are not the noblest goals." This is true. The question now becomes, what is your goal? Do you even have a clearly stated goal? Do you have this singleness of purpose that gives focus to a person's life and allows him or her to excel beyond imagining?

This singleness of purpose will save you from wasting your life in shallow and superficial activities that mean almost nothing to anyone, anywhere, and will mean even less one hundred years from now. Imagine how many people wanted to distract Michael Jordan from practicing his basketball. Imagine how many nights his friends wanted him to go out and party and he didn't, either because he had to practice or because he had to get up early the next morning and practice. Imagine how many people tried to distract Bill Gates from building Microsoft in his late teens and early twenties. Similarly, imagine how many people tried to distract Mother Teresa from her prayer time or from her work with the poorest of the poor.

When you have singleness of purpose, everything else is embraced or discarded according to whether or not it moves you in the direction of your goal. When you don't have this singleness of purpose, you get lost in the tossing and turning of daily life.

For the man who knows where he is going, the whole world will get out of the way. For those who do not, the world becomes a playground filled with nothingness.

It was precisely with this in mind that Ignatius of Loyola established his First Principle and Foundation:

"Man is created to praise, reverence, and serve God our Lord, and by this means to save his soul.

The other things on the face of the earth are created for man to help him in attaining the end for which he is created.

Hence, man is to make use of them in as far as they help him in the attainment of his end, and he must rid himself of them in as far as they prove a hindrance to him.

Therefore, we must make ourselves indifferent to all created things, as far as we are allowed free choice and are not under any prohibition. Consequently, as far as we are concerned, we should not prefer health to sickness, riches to poverty, honor to dishonor, a long life to a short life. The same holds for all other things.

Our one desire and choice should be what is more conducive to the end for which we are created."

———

So what will be your goal? Upon what will you fix yourself with singleness of purpose? All of Bill Gates' work and money have value only inasmuch as they help him to become the-best-version-of-himself. All of Michael Jordan's training and playing, fame and fortune have value only inasmuch as they help him become the-best-version-of-himself. Mother Teresa has chosen the better path and the ultimate goal. She fixed her singleness of purpose on sanctity. What does it mean? To become a saint. What does that mean? To become the-best-version-of-yourself, to become all God created you to be.

This singleness of purpose, this goal, is very important. Everyday you and I make hundreds of decisions, some of them large and some of them small. If you have this singleness of purpose, decision-making becomes much easier. The saints simply asked themselves, "Will this help me become the-best-version-of-myself?" If they concluded that it would help them become the-best-version-of-themselves, then they embraced it. If they decided that it wouldn't, then they turned their backs on it, regardless of how alluring the opportunity was. That is the value of singleness of purpose.

The Will of God

The saints perfectly aligned themselves with the will of God. That is what makes them saints – this synthesis of their own individual will and the will of God. In this modern era, people have been seduced by the dark lie that it is impossible to know the will of God. This is a diabolical lie of unfathomable proportions, because it separates us from our essential purpose and leads us down a road to misery and despair.

The will of God is that you become the-best-version-of-yourself. God doesn't want to control you, or manipulate you, or stifle you, or force you to do things you don't want to do. If that were God's desire, then he would not have given you free will in the first place. God wants you to become all you can be, and in the process he wants you to experience the greatest mystery of them all – love. God invites you to embark on the adventure of unveiling and actualizing your unimagined potential. This is the adventure of salvation – and we make this journey by learning to love God, neighbor, self, and indeed, life. This is the Journey of the Soul, the adventure of salvation, and the quest for love.

The will of God is not as mysterious as many make it out to be. You come home from work and you have a choice: you can sit on the couch in front of the TV with a large bag of potato chips and some beer, or you can go for a run. Which will help you become the-best-version-of-yourself? Every situation can be approached with this question.

In his first letter to the Thessalonians, Paul addresses this same question, writing, "This is the will of God:

that you be saints" (1 Thessalonians 3:4). God wants you to be a saint, and it is critical for modern Catholics to hear this call to sanctity once again. We must all be reminded that holiness is within our reach. We must teach and proclaim that the will of God can be discovered and embraced. But for this to happen, we must set aside our prejudices against the idea of holiness and embrace a new vision of holiness.

The caricatures of holiness that modern society has created and ridiculed are not authentic models of holiness. A man or a woman becoming the-best-version-of-himself or herself – that is holiness. The world and the Church are desperately in need of this authentic striving for holiness.

As we discussed earlier, holiness is as simple as knowing when to say "yes" and when to say "no." But in order to say no to anything, you have to have a *deeper yes*. That is what is missing in most people's lives, this *deeper yes*. Defining our goal – to become the-best-version-of-ourselves, to become saints – creates a singleness of purpose and the *deeper yes* necessary to turn our backs on so many of the self-destructive and superficial activities of this modern culture.

This is precisely what sets the saints apart from the masses of humanity marching through history. They fixed their gaze on God. They resolved to do God's will. They discovered their essential purpose, and they fixed the attention of their thoughts, words, and actions on the great Spiritual North Star. They sought to do only the will of God, and as a result, they blossomed and bloomed to become all God had created them to be. That is the value of singleness of purpose, and it is written on each of their lives.

One of my favorite passages from the Bible affirms my belief that the will of God is not as much of a mystery as we make it out to be at times. It comes from the book of Micah, "You have been told what is good and what Yahweh wants of you. Only this, that you live justly, love tenderly, and walk humbly with your God" (Micah 6:8).

In my own life, I know justice from injustice. We are able to recognize the difference when we see it in our daily lives. We may not always behave justly, but we know the just path even when we do not choose it. We know what is just and what is not in the circumstances of our own lives. We may not know what is just and right in matters of international politics, but few of us are in positions that require us to make those decisions. The same God who shows you what is just and unjust in your life also shows presidents, kings, and commanders what is just and unjust. The challenge is not in the knowing. Our hearts are faithful in directing us when we listen. The challenge is in surrendering our prideful and selfish wills to the will of God.

The second directive from this passage in Micah is that we love tenderly. In the same way we know what is just, we know also how to love. In every situation, we can choose love or selfishness, love or pride, love or gluttony, love or jealousy, love or lust... We know how to love tenderly.

Finally, the prophet speaks of walking humbly with God. It is cited last, but it is in fact first, because it is this walking humbly with God that makes justice and love possible in our lives. It is allowing God as your Father to take you by the hand and lead you. But too often we want to race off ahead of our Father, tearing our hand out of his and running frantically in all directions. We don't want to miss anything. We want to experience everything that this life has to offer so we run here and there in search of happiness. If we would just walk humbly with our God, he would lead us by the hand to that which is just for us, made for us, intended for us, and this alone will be the cause of our deep fulfillment and happiness.

But, this walking humbly with God is difficult. To achieve this humble walk with God, we must acquire the habits of recollection and self-possession. Let me use another illustration to further our understanding of this point. How hard is it to walk humbly with God? It is as if I lit a candle and gave it to you to hold, and told you to take it everywhere you go and never let it be blown out. You would have to protect it, wouldn't you? You would have to move slowly, thoughtfully, deliberately.

This is what is required to walk humbly with God. The candle is within you. When you have learned to carry and protect it, then you will be able to live justly – choose what is good, just, true, and noble in every situation - and love tenderly.

The candle is within you. Protect it. Don't let the world blow it out.

The will of God is that you become the-best-version-of-yourself, or in classical spiritual language, that you become a saint. You become the-best-version-of-yourself by applying your singleness of purpose to the great Spiritual North Star, and one by one, forming the habits that will perfect your character.

How Would You Like Your Life to Change?

Apart from this singleness of purpose, there is one other sign that separates men and women of extraordinary achievement from those who get devoured by mediocrity and superficiality. While some may still be arguing that the difference between those who excel and those who don't is luck or chance, I can tell you with absolute certainty that it is not. This is the difference: they just have better habits. If you dissect their lives, you discover that they fill their days, weeks, and months with habits that are helping them to become the-best-version-of-themselves, while most people fill their lives with habits that are self-destructive.

What are your habits? What are the things you do everyday, every week, or every month? If you can tell me what your habits are, I can tell you what sort of a person you are. How? Habits create character. Good habits create good character, and bad habits create bad character.

What are your habits? If you can tell me what your habits are, I can tell you what your future looks like. How? Habits create character, and your character is your destiny. Good habits create good character, which in turn creates a wonderful future. Bad habits create bad character, which in turn creates misery in your future.

Habits create character, and your character is your destiny. Your character is your destiny in the work place, your character is your destiny in relationships, and your character is your destiny in eternity.

The good news is, we can change our habits.

What new habits are you trying to form in your life right now? If you can tell me what new habits you are trying to form in your life right now, I can tell you how your future will be different from your past. Why? Our lives change when our habits change.

How would you like your life to be different this year than it was last year? And how do you hope for this change to come about? Most people live in the miscredited fantasy that one-day they will wake up, and all of a sudden their lives will be magically different. It never happens. They grow old and die wishing. Others live in the illusion that if they make more money, or get a new car, or a bigger house, or a promotion, or vacation in the Bahamas – then their lives will change. This doesn't work either.

Our lives change when our habits change.

———

Take a few minutes right now. Put this book down. Find a piece of paper and write down a list of your habits. Think about it. What are the things you do everyday, every week, or every month? Now go down the list and ask yourself, which of these habits are helping me to become the-best-version-of-myself? And which of the habits are self-destructive?

Now... you tell me, what sort of a person are you? What does your future look like?

———

If you want your future to be different from your past, there is only one way. Change your habits. Our lives change when our habits change. Essentially, that is what sets the heroes, leaders, champions, and saints apart from the rest. They just had better habits. Their habits were not the self-destructive type that we effortlessly pick up by traveling the path of least resistance. Their habits were helping them to become the-best-version-of-themselves, and they were acquired intentionally by the effort of discipline.

CHAPTER TEN

THEIR ATTRACTION & INFLUENCE

There is nothing more beautiful in this life than a good friendship. When I was a teenager, my father held out his hand, spread his five fingers wide, and said to me, "If you find five true friends in your lifetime, you will have lived a life infinitely blessed." At the time, I thought it was a little strange because I had so many friends, but as the years have passed, my father's wisdom has become more and more apparent.

Friendship

The question I have struggled with over the years is, What constitutes a true friend? Perhaps it would be helpful for you to pause for a moment and reflect. Who are your true friends? What makes them good friends?

As a child, I thought friendship was about hanging out together all the time and sticking up for each other when others were critical or cruel. In my adolescence, I thought a true friend was someone who liked everything you liked and never did anything to upset you. But as an adult, I have learned that the defining quality of a true friendship is when the other person encourages you to be all you can be, challenges you to become the-best-version-of-yourself, and vice versa.

What sort of people do you like being with? What types of people give you energy?

As I look at my life and my years of traveling, there are certain people who I yearn to spend time with. Some days, as I walk through the airport and look at the television monitors to see which gate my flight is leaving from, I look at the list of cities and one will catch my eye. For a moment, I wish I were going to that city. Why? Because there is someone in that city who inspires and energizes me to be all I can be.

I love being around people who are constantly striving to better themselves. They energize me. They inspire me. They challenge me. They make me want to be a better person.

This is true friendship. A true friend brings the best out of her friends.

For this reason, when I have time to spend with friends socially, I try to surround myself with people who make me want to be a better person. I admit they are not easy to find, but when you do find them, they are more precious than any treasure or pleasure this world has to offer.

If you want a litmus test for choosing friends, use this question: Will spending time with this person make me want to be a better person?

Spiritual Friends & Loneliness

I try to apply this truth not only to my social life, but also to my spiritual life. This is why the saints are such good friends. They challenge us to become all we can be and encourage us to become the-best-version-of-ourselves. But the real beauty is found in their method. They don't preach endless sermons, and they don't try to impose their views on others – they challenge, inspire, and encourage us simply by living their own lives to the fullest. That is the social dynamic of holiness. It is attractive, and it is contagious.

If you and I sit down at lunch and you order soup and a salad, it makes me think twice about ordering a double cheeseburger with bacon and fries. If my friends are going to the gym after work, I feel that inner nudge to work out myself. If a colleague is honest and humble about a mistake he has made, I am humbled by his example of humility.

Goodness is contagious. The problem is, so is evil. The challenge for you and me, as Christians in the midst of the modern world, is to be examples of good living.

None of us realize how much we influence others. Everything you do, people are watching, and everything you say, people are listening. The influence of your words and actions is contributing to the way they live their lives. In *A Call to Joy,* I wrote, "You will learn more from your friends than you ever will from books. Choose your friends wisely."

This is why the saints are such treasures. They may have lived in another place and time, but they can be true friends. I'd rather spend a couple of hours with

Francis of Assisi and Teresa of Avila than with some of my contemporaries on a Friday night getting drunk. I'd much rather spend time with dead people who inspire me to be all I can be than with live people who lead me to be just a shadow of all God created me to be.

I promise you, it is better to spend time with dead people who bring you to life than with live people who lead you to death.

From time to time, I meet people who are dating a person they know they don't want to spend the rest of their lives with. If you ask them why, they say it is because they don't like being alone. I have learned it is better to be alone than with the wrong person.

Don't be afraid of your loneliness. Use it as an opportunity to befriend people who inspire you. Harness your loneliness as a chance to befriend the saints.

Foster this Spirit

The one quality we should try to develop is this striving to better ourselves. Each morning when I am showering, I ask myself the same question: What will it take today for me to become the better person I know I can be? Then I go through the four major areas of life: physical, emotional, intellectual, and spiritual. In each of these areas, I try to focus on one thing I can do that day to grow.

It is the transformation that energizes us and fills our lives with passion and enthusiasm.

Focus on developing the spirit of transformation in your life. When you are choosing friends, choose those who are striving to better themselves. And if you are young and single, and sense you are called to marriage, seek a soul mate, a spouse, a companion for the journey who has this quality.

Bright Lights

The saints were remarkable men and women, but surprisingly what made them remarkable was rarely anything too spectacular. What made them extraordinary was the ordinary. In the ordinary things of everyday life, they strove to grow in virtue. If they were caring for the sick, they were growing in humility. When they were educating the children, they were growing in patience.

There is something ultimately attractive about holiness. When holiness emerges in any place and time, all men and women of good will are inspired. What is it that makes them so attractive? The saints want to improve themselves. It is this one quality that is incredibly attractive and ultimately inspiring. They are not proud and arrogant about who they are and what they have done. They are focused on becoming the-best-version-of-themselves. They are striving with all their might to become the better people they know they can be. All their time, effort, and energy are focused on becoming perfectly the person God created them to be.

Recently, I walked into a bookstore, and sitting on the shelves in the front of the store, were several large coffee-table type books. One of them caught my eye, so I walked over to have a look. For the next ten minutes, I flipped through the pages of two books, glancing at the pictures, and a great fire was fanned in my heart. One was about the life of Mother Teresa and the other about the life of John Paul II. The world has a great need for the example of authentic lives because we all need to be inspired. We need to be reminded of what is possible. These people have allowed God to fill them with his love, and the glow of that love alive in them is blinding. The power of their lives and the greatness of their spirits cannot be adequately put into words. But occasionally, in the memory of an event in their lives, or in the story a photo tells, we catch a glimpse.

Just passing through those pages, glancing at the pictures, my heart was elevated and my spirit began to soar. Just looking at those pictures made me want to be a better person. I didn't even read a word. That is the power of these great lives.

They are the personification of that phrase from Matthew's Gospel - *Luceat Lux Vestra* – "Let your light shine" (Matthew 5:16). And because they have allowed God to shine so powerfully through them, men and women of all faiths gasp in awe of their presence.

Even a blind man knows when he is in the presence of a bright light.

There is nothing more attractive than holiness. Throughout history, wherever men and women of holiness have lived, the Church has blossomed and bloomed. This is the answer to all of our questions and the solution to all of our problems – holiness of life.

CHAPTER ELEVEN

WHO WILL BE NEXT?

The stage is set.

The modern world awaits the emergence of a handful of spiritual heroes and heroines who will inspire and mobilize the masses toward a more Christ-centered way of living.

The fruit is ripe on the vine.

The question is not, *Will* God raise up great saints in our own day and age? The question is, *Who* will God raise up? And the answer: those you least expect.

Throughout history, the great transformations and movements within the Church have always come from outside the expected channels. First man creates a problem, and then God, in his infinite wisdom, creates a solution. If the problems today are greater than ever before, then God will raise up saints greater than ever before.

You can be certain of one thing. As dark and as grim as things may seem for the Church at times, these circumstances will conspire to produce a group of modern saints. God will use these circumstances to call forth men and women who will shadow the saints of ages past.

The Church needs saints, and the world needs saints – people willing to acknowledge God's will for their own lives, men and women dedicated to prayer and striving for virtue. We need great spiritual masters to teach us the way of holiness.

Beyond the Church, our whole culture is desperately in need of a return to virtue. But apart from striving for virtue in our own lives, how can we help God raise up this next generation of spiritual leaders?

To Whom Does the Future Belong?

As we look at where we are and where we are going, both as a Church and as a human family, we should ask ourselves, Who and what will be the greatest influences in determining the future? To whom does the future belong? What will the future be like?

The most powerful and influential position in any society or civilization is as a storyteller. These storytellers are not just the mythical cultural icons who dress up on Thursday afternoons and read stories to your children in local libraries and bookstores. Musicians are storytellers, and politicians are storytellers. Screenplay writers are storytellers, and business leaders are storytellers. Teachers, preachers, nurses, lawyers, pastors, priests, scientists, salespeople, artists, mothers, fathers, poets, philosophers, brothers, sisters, baby-sitters, grandparents... we are all story-tellers.

The future belongs to the storytellers. The future belongs to us. What will the future be like? Well, that depends very much on the stories we tell, the stories we listen to, and the stories we live.

Stories have a remarkable ability to cut through the clutter and confusion and bring clarity to our hearts and minds. Stories remind us of our values, aims, and goals. Stories sneak beyond the boundaries of our prej-udices to soften our hearts to a new truth. Great peri-ods in history emerge when great stories are told and lived. Stories are history that form the future. Stories are prophecies set in the past.

Stories are important.

Stories are as essential as the air we breathe and the water we drink. Stories captivate our imaginations, enchant our minds, and empower our spirits. Stories introduce us to who we are and who we are capable of being. Stories change our lives.

If you wish to poison a nation, poison the stories that nation listens to. If you wish to win people over to your team or to your point of view, do not go to war or argue with them – tell them a story.

All great leaders understand the persuasive and inspirational power of stories. When did you last hear a great speech that didn't contain a story?

A story can do anything: win a war, lose a war, heal the sick, encourage the discouraged, comfort the oppressed, inspire a revolution, transform an enemy into a friend, elevate the consciousness of the people, build empires, inspire love, even reshape the spiritual temperament of a whole age.

Sixty-five percent of the Gospels are stories – parables. The other thirty-five percent is the story of Jesus Christ.

We are the storytellers. What type of stories are we telling? I promise you with absolute certitude - the future depends on the stories we tell. The future belongs to the storytellers. What will your story be?

Shame on Us

If we wish to raise up a new generation of saints, there are two indispensable ingredients. In the first place, always in the first place, we must strive to grow in holiness, to become more perfectly the person God created us to be. And secondly, we must tell the stories of the champions and heroes of our faith that have gone before us.

There is no medium more powerful than stories to convey a message. We have the stories, but we are not conveying them. Our two-thousand-year Catholic history is full of extraordinary stories about ordinary people who opened their hearts to God and allowed the life, teachings, and person of Jesus Christ to transform their lives. These men and women are the heroes and heroines of our faith; they are a rare gift of inspiration, and we have failed as a Church to tell their stories. Shame on us.

Pick up a copy of a photo book about John Paul II. Don't even read the words; just look at the pictures, and you will have goose bumps. Pick up a book about

Mother Teresa and flip through the photos, and you will have a tingling sensation up and down your spine. Read George Weigel's biography of John Paul II and you will have a life-changing experience. Read Robert Bolt's *A Man for All Seasons* or watch the movie, and you will be challenged to become the-best-version-of-yourself. Read your children stories of the saints.

It is true our modern culture is guilty of telling horrific and disdainful stories that promote violence, sexual promiscuity, and every manner of sin known to man. It is true that the modern media has launched an attack on Catholicism at this time in history. It is also true that in this age of anti-prejudice, the only socially acceptable prejudice is to be anti-Catholic. But we have contributed to all these problems because, as a family of faith, we are guilty of not telling the great stories of our spiritual ancestors – the saints.

The lives of the saints are stories of virtue and character, and if we would tell them and listen to them, our lives would become examples of that same virtue and character.

We become the stories we tell. We become the stories we listen to.

What Are You Willing to Give Your Life For?

I once heard a story about Abraham Lincoln during the war. He had called for one of the men under his command who had an excellent reputation. Lincoln needed the soldier to deliver a message to another battalion that was dangerously positioned on the other side of the enemy. If both battalions could be coordinated to attack the opposition at the same time, their position would become a strategic advantage.

When the young man arrived, without disclosing the nature of the assignment, Lincoln explained that he had a very dangerous mission and asked the soldier if he would be willing to take on such a commission. He said, "I am willing to die for our cause." Lincoln replied, "I have 25,000 men who are willing to die for the cause. What I need is one who is willing to live for it."

At different times in the history of Christianity, men and women have had to die for their faith. Our own times are not in need of people willing to die for the faith. What the modern Church desperately needs is men and women who are willing to live for the faith.

What are you willing to live for?

Just before her death, Joan of Arc wrote, "I know this now. Every man gives his life for what he believes. Every woman gives her life for what she believes. Sometimes people believe in little or nothing, and yet they give their lives to that little or nothing. One life is all we have, and we live it as we believe in living it and then it's gone. But to surrender what you are and to live without belief is more terrible than dying – even more terrible than dying young."

What are you willing to give your life for? There are two ways to interpret the question, but I am not asking what are you willing to die for. I am wondering, what are you willing to live for? What are you willing to give your life for? Not in death or martyrdom, but in life.

What great cause are you willing to support with the moments of your life?

On September 11, 2001, we learned a lesson that history has taught us many times before. The most powerful people in history are those who are willing to give everything.

The nineteen hijackers were willing to give everything to complete their mission. In every age, on both sides of the fence of good and evil, the most powerful agents of change are those people willing to give all their time, effort, and energy without reserve to the cause they deem worthy of their lives. We saw this in the hijackers and we saw this in Hitler, but we also see it in Mother Teresa, Francis of Assisi, Ignatius of Loyola, and countless other heroic men and women throughout history who have given their lives to the service of God, humanity, and the Gospel. The question I ask again is, What are *you* willing to give *your* life for?

Perhaps a better place to start is with the question, What are you giving your life to? When you assess the way you spend your days and weeks, to what are you contributing your time, efforts, energy, and talents?

As a teenager, I used to play a lot of golf at a club not far from where we lived. I remember how some men used to spend their whole lives at the golf club. There were one or two in particular whose whole lives seemed to revolve around the life of the club. They would play, but they were also on the board. They would hang around in the restaurant or the bar, and from time to time, I would even see them pulling weeds or trimming bushes in the gardens that surrounded the first tee. Even as a child, I remember thinking that there must be something lacking in them to spend their lives this way. But I suppose we all need something to live for, something to get out of bed for each day, and for them it was the golf club.

Do you ever think about dying? Whenever I am exposed to the reality and inevitability of death, it always heightens my awareness of how brief and precious our time here on Earth is. Sometimes it is the death of a friend, at other times it is a news story, or perhaps just a bumpy ride on a plane. These events help me to treasure my own life more and more with each passing day. But they also challenge me to reassess the way I am spending the time, effort, and energies that are my life. I am more intimately aware than ever before that we all waste life. We waste it one day at time, a day here and a day there. We waste some days caught up in unforgiveness, and we waste other days immersed in frivolous and irresponsible activities.

Life is passing us by. Life is wonderful but brief, and yet, filled with unimaginable potential. Within each of us, there is a light. It is the light of God, and when it shines, it reflects not only the wonder of God, but also the greatness of the human spirit. We live in difficult times. I pray that we never become fearful, but rather, that we turn our focus to nurturing the light within us. I hope we allow that light within us to be nourished and to grow. Darkness has one enemy that it can never defeat – light.

Let your light shine!

As we reflect on our brief and precious lives, let us also remember that they are but a transition to a long and blissful eternity. Teresa of Avila reminds us,

"Remember you have only one soul; that you have only one death to die; that you have only one life, which is short and has to be lived by you alone; and there is only one glory, which is eternal. If you do this, there will be a great many things about which you care nothing."

Finding Your Place

What you must do is find your place in the history of humanity. You see the world doesn't need another Mother Teresa. The Church doesn't need another Francis of Assisi. The world needs you. The Church needs you. Mother Teresa had a role to play in God's plan, and she played it. Francis had a mission in God's plan, and he fulfilled it. Now you must find your role, your place. Who will be next? You. You will be next if you make yourself available to God completely and unconditionally.

Find your place in salvation history. Be yourself. Perfectly yourself. Be a saint.

The best thing you can do for *yourself* is become the-best-version-of-yourself.

The best thing you can do for *your spouse* is become the-best-version-of-yourself.

The best thing you can do for *your children* is become the-best-version-of-yourself.

The best thing you can do for *your friends* is become the-best-version-of-yourself.

The best thing you can do for *your Church* is become the-best-version-of-yourself.

The best thing you can do for *your nation* is become the-best-version-of-yourself.

The best thing you can do for *God* is become the-best-version-of-yourself.

———

Catholicism is not a lifeless set of rules and regulations. Catholicism is a lifestyle. Catholicism is a way of life designed by God to help you become all you can be.

Where Do We Start?

We are at a turning point in human history. Most people do not recognize it because they are so consumed with their own selfish desires and the trivial happenings of their daily lives. Nonetheless, we are at a turning point in history. What is needed is a handful of great spiritual leaders to direct the human family during this critical period of transition. The modern Western Empire is in decline. It will soon die. It's not the end of the world. It's not the end of humanity. It's just the beginning of a new era. A new civilization will emerge. What will this new civilization be like? That is entirely up to the stories we tell, listen to, and live.

Cardinal Ratzinger says, "the crucial question is whether there are saints who... are ready to effect something new and living." As Christians, we are called to holiness – a life of prayer and virtue. We are called to be saints. May God grant us generous spirits.

This commission is certainly a great task. A little self-reflection signals to us clearly how far we have to go. But do not allow yourself to become discouraged. Familiarize yourself with the lives of the saints. They were not born saints. They did not become saints overnight. In most cases, they didn't set out to do anything extraordinary, and they didn't set out to change the world. These extraordinary souls were very much focused on the ordinary. They allowed the everyday activities of their lives to transform them. They saw every event as an opportunity to grow in virtue. And as a result, they lived extraordinary lives that inspired the people of their time and the people of centuries to come. They may seem larger than life, but most of them found their greatness by performing their daily duties with love.

Who will be next? You. You and me I pray. Where do we start? At the beginning, with ourselves, today. Francis of Assisi shared the secret with his brothers and sisters saying, "First do what is necessary. Then do what is possible. And before you know it, you will be doing the impossible."

If not you, then who? What will your excuse be? What are you afraid of? What is holding you back from being all you can be?

On May 10, 1994, the world celebrated as a black man was inaugurated as the President of a country that had been the strongest symbol of racial oppression for decades. Just four years earlier, he had been released from prison, having served more than twenty years. As he stepped to the podium that day the whole world was listening and the words he spoke to the people of South Africa reached into the hearts of people everywhere. They are timeless words with infinite relevance for our own lives.

"Our deepest fear is not that we are inadequate. Our deepest fear is that we are powerful beyond measure. It is our light, not our darkness that most frightens us. We ask ourselves, Who am I to be brilliant, gorgeous, talented and fabulous? Actually, Who are you not to be? You are a child of God. Your playing small doesn't serve the world. There is nothing enlightened about shrinking so that other people won't feel insecure around you. We are born to make manifest the glory of God that is within us. It is not just in some of us, it is in everyone. And as we let our own light shine, we unconsciously give other people permission to do the same. As we are liberated from our own fear, our presence automatically liberates others."

—◆◆—

If you could change anything about the world, what would you change?

The world is the way it is today because of people like you and me. Our thoughts, words, actions, and inaction have all contributed to create the world of today.

What sort of world would it be if we multiplied your life by six billion?

Whatever change you desire for the world, create that change in your own life. You are here for a purpose. Seek out your purpose. Hunt your purpose down. The greatest misery is to be purposeless. The great depression of our age is not economic, but spiritual. Our spiritual poverty is rooted in our purposelessness.

As I have written the pages that make up this chapter, the words of John Henry Newman have been echoing in my heart:

"God has created me to do him some definite service. He has committed some work to me which he has not committed to another. I have my mission. I may never know it in this life, but I shall be told it in the next. I am a link in a chain, a bond of connection between persons. He has not created me for naught. I shall do good – I shall do his work. I shall be an angel of peace, a preacher of truth in my own place while not intending it, if I do but keep his commandments. Therefore I will trust him, whatever I am, I can never be thrown away. If I am in sickness, my sickness may serve him. In perplexity, my perplexity may serve him. If I am in sorrow, my sorrow may serve him. He does nothing in vain. He knows what he is about. He may take away my friends. He may throw me among strangers. He may make me feel desolate, make my spirits sink, hide my future from me – still, HE KNOWS WHAT HE IS ABOUT."

―――

Only one thing is necessary for Catholicism to flourish – authentic lives. Throughout history, wherever you find men and women genuinely striving to live the Christian life, the Church has always blossomed. If we wish to speak effectively to the modern world about God, the Christian life, and the Catholic Church, we must be thriving, blossoming, and flourishing in that life.

PART THREE

THE SEVEN PILLARS OF
CATHOLIC SPIRITUALITY

It strikes me with alarming importance that in the course of the entire Gospels, the disciples make only one request of Jesus: "Lord, teach us to pray" (John 11:1).

The people of every age yearn for God. We have a longing to be nearer to God, a desire to be in communion with him. The request modern Catholics have of Jesus alive in the Church today is the very same request: "Teach us to pray."

The great tragedy of modern Catholicism is that, as Catholics, we are not considered a spiritual people. If you polled people on the streets and asked them to list five words to describe Catholics, I suspect only a very small minority would ascribe the quality "spiritual." The tragedy, however, is not how people perceive Catholics, but the fact that the perception may reflect the reality. It is a generalization, but as Catholics in this modern climate, we tend not to take our spirituality seriously.

The Seven Pillars of Catholic Spirituality that we will discuss in this section combine two thousand years of spiritual wisdom into a handful of spiritual exercises. Is it merely a coincidence that you find these Seven Pillars so common to the lives of the saints? Is it not a logical and reasonable conclusion that, if we apply these practices to our own lives, we will grow in holiness?

Our spiritual heritage is rich in wisdom and practice. If we can embrace this spiritual heritage and adapt it to the modern context, we will begin again to thrive as the spiritual people God intended us to be.

CHAPTER TWELVE

RECONCILIATION

Over the past fifteen years, I have been amazed at the emergence and dominance of two great sporting figures. Michael Jordan and Tiger Woods are arguably the greatest sportsmen in history. You may be wondering what these icons of modern sport have to do with Catholicism. Stay with me, I assure you I have a point.

What intrigues me about the success Jordan and Woods have enjoyed is that the same quality that makes Michael Jordan the greatest basketball player in history is also the quality that makes Tiger Woods the greatest golfer. They play two very different sports that require very different skills and disciplines, yet all their success can be linked to a singular quality. Let me explain.

As a teenager growing up in North Carolina, Michael Jordan couldn't even make the high-school basketball team. Now he is the greatest basketball player in history. How does that happen? Some people would tell you it was mere luck or freak talent. Others will tell you he is one of God's favored few or he was in the right place and had the right opportunities. None of these are true.

In high school, Michael Jordan trained harder and longer than anyone else on the team or on the bench. With hard work, he increased his skills and earned his place. When he made it to college basketball, his percentages from the free-throw line were weak. So, for almost ten years, Jordan made more than five hundred free throws everyday. He didn't shoot five hundred shots, he made five hundred. When would you next go to bed if you couldn't go to bed until you'd made five hundred free throws? Similarly, when Jordan entered the NBA, he felt that his fade-away jump shot was weak. So he focused his practice on his fade-away jump shot until it became one of the high points of his game.

In 1997, Tiger Woods won the Masters by a record number of strokes. In the world's most prestigious golfing event, the twenty-one year old demolished a world-class field in such a fashion that many began to wonder whether golf would be competitive anymore. Only weeks later, Woods and his coach announced at a press conference that he was going to take some time off. During that time, he explained, he and his coach intended to completely deconstruct and reconstruct his golf swing. Baffled, the international press asked, why? Woods explained that, with the help of his coach and video footage of his swing, they had discovered a fault, which they believed would not stand up under the pressure of a tight match. Within a couple of months, Woods returned to the tour with his new swing to completely dominate the sport like no one else in history.

Both Michael Jordan and Tiger Woods have an incredible ability to look at their game and establish their strengths and their weaknesses. Once they have done this, they work tirelessly to transform their weaknesses into strengths.

Where did they get this idea? Is it something Michael Jordan came up with and handed on to Tiger Woods? Is it an idea that has just been born in the last twenty-five years?

This process of identifying strengths and weaknesses, and transforming weaknesses into strengths, is at the core of Catholic spirituality. For two thousand years, the men and women we call saints have been going into the Classroom of Silence, taking a humble and honest look at themselves, and assessing their strengths and weaknesses. Then, armed with that knowledge, they have bravely set forth to transform their weaknesses into strengths - their vices into virtues. In the Classroom of Silence, they didn't reflect on their basketball game or their golf swing, they reflected on their character. Their transformation was the most important of all – the inner transformation.

They understood that who we become is infinitely more important than what we do or what we have.

What are your weaknesses? Do you know? Most people don't want to think about their weaknesses. We don't want to talk about them, and we certainly don't want anyone else to point them out. This is a classic sign of mediocrity. Great men and women want to know their weaknesses.

Your weaknesses are the keys to your richer, more abundant future. Your strengths are probably already bearing the fruit they can. They will continue to bear those good fruits in your life, but the plateau effect will set in. It is unlikely they will bear more fruit. Your richer, more abundant future is intimately linked to your weaknesses. By transforming your weaknesses into strengths, the gifts God wants to endow you with will begin to expand.

Turning to God

When John the Baptist first appeared in the desert of Judea, this was his message: "Repent, for the kingdom of heaven is at hand" (Matthew 3:2). Later, when Jesus began his ministry, he also led with this message: "Repent, for the kingdom of heaven is at hand" (Matthew 5:17).

Repent is a powerful word. But what does it mean for you and me, here and now, two thousand years later? It means the same as it did to the people walking around the dusty pathways in their sandals, trying to inch closer to Jesus as he passed through their town or village. Repent means to turn back to God. Do you need to?

We often turn away from God. Sometimes in small ways, just for a moment, and at other times it is in larger ways. Turning our backs on God is an inner action. It is quite possible for people to turn their backs on

God and still go to church every Sunday. The external actions don't guarantee the internal disposition. What is missing is growth in virtue. Have you turned your back on God in some area of your life?

Every journey toward something is a journey away from something. If we need to turn back to God at this moment in our lives, we also need to turn away from whatever has led us away from God. Maybe some people have led you to stray from God, perhaps possessions have distracted you from the straight and narrow road, or maybe pleasures have seduced you into walking a wayward path. Whatever has distracted you, it is important to realize that you cannot journey to a new place and at the same time stay where you are.

The journey toward the-best-version-of-yourself is a journey away from the defects of the-present-version-of-yourself. The question that really presents itself to you, me, and to this modern age collectively is: Are you willing to turn back to God?

I am a Sinner

Everyday, I find myself doing things that are self-destructive and make me a lesser person. I find myself saying things that hurt others, or hurting others by not saying things. On those days, you can be sure the things I am thinking are giving birth to those words and actions. These are thoughts, words, and actions that deviate from the natural order and separate me from the peace of knowing I am contributing positively to the common good of the unfolding universe.

The strange thing is, deep within me I don't want to think, say, and do these things. I don't want to be the lesser person; I want to be the better person I know I can be. I want to live by contributing to other people's happiness, not their misery. In each moment of each day, I find myself caught in a struggle. I am divided. No different from you, I find myself experiencing what Paul described, "The good that I would I do not, and the evil that I would not it is that which I do" (Romans 7:19).

I am a sinner. This is what makes me eligible for membership in the Catholic Church. Jesus didn't come for the healthy, he came for the sick, and he established the Church to continue his work (cf. Mark 2:17). I am imperfect, but capable of change and growth. Imperfect, but perfectible. The Church holds me in my weakness, comforts me in my limitations, endeavors to heal me of my sickness, and nurtures me back to full health – making me "whole" again.

The Drama of Life

Over the past ten years, I have written and spoken extensively about what I like to call "the Journey of the Soul." In *The Rhythm of Life,* I describe it as a journey from Point A to Point B. Point A represents the person you are today, and Point B represents the-best-version-of-yourself. This journey is the adventure of salvation. The whole drama of a person's life can be understood by examining the tension between the-person-I-am and the-person-I-ought-to-be. This is the tension of life. And it is the resolution of this tension that Paul spoke of when he suggested we must each work out our salvation (cf. Philippians 2:12).

The great Spiritual North Star – God's invitation to holiness - calls us toward Point B. Everything has its meaning in relation to the goal, and when we forget the goal, nothing makes sense. When we lose sight of the great Spiritual North Star, we become lost and confused. This is why Catholicism means so little to so many today, because they have forgotten, or in some cases have never been introduced to, the goal of the Christian life.

Everything should be weighed with the journey in mind and the goal in sight. The question that should be a consistent part of our inner dialogue is, "Will what I am about to do help me become the-best-version-of-myself?"

This is the drama of life – the struggle to become the-best-version-of-myself, the quest to bridge the gap between the-person-I-am and the-person-I-ought-to-be.

The Sacramental Setting

It is within this context that I wish to speak to you about the beauty of the sacrament of Reconciliation. In my own personal journey, Reconciliation has played a very powerful role helping me to strive to become the-best-version-of-myself. I find Reconciliation to be a humbling experience, but not a humiliating one. Above all, I find it to be an experience of liberation that enables me to reassess where I am in the journey, helps me to identify what is holding me back, and encourages me to continue along the way. Reconciliation is much more than just confessing our sins and asking for forgiveness. It is part of the genius of Catholicism, which seeks to nurture the whole person.

While any spiritual exercise can be helpful in this journey, I find Reconciliation to be a particularly powerful tool. As I have traveled the world, it has become apparent that this sacrament has been abandoned during our own time. I believe this has happened because a tragic mediocrity has gripped the Church.

People striving to excel in any area of life want to know their weaknesses so they can work to overcome them. This striving for excellence is precisely what needs to be re-ignited in Catholics today. Reconciliation is the perfect spiritual tool to re-ignite our passion for excellence in the spiritual life.

When I close my eyes in prayer, I see the-person-I-am and the-best-version-of-myself side by side, and I am challenged to change. This is what takes place in Reconciliation. We prepare by asking ourselves some soul-searching questions. Those questions give birth to the dual vision of the person we are at this moment and the person we are capable of becoming. We then bring our faults, failings, flaws, and defects to God. In return, he gives us the mysterious gift of grace – the desire and the strength to grow and become the-best-version-of-ourselves.

Grace heals the wounds that our sins have created. Grace helps us to maintain moral balance. Grace helps us to persevere in the pursuit of virtue. Grace enlightens our minds to see and know which actions will help us become all God has created us to be. Grace inspires us to love what is good and shun what is evil. Grace is not a magical illusion, grace is mystical and real. Grace is the power of God alive within us.

I come to this sacrament to reconcile with myself, my imperfection, God, and the community. Reconciliation is not just a cleansing experience, but also a strengthening experience.

Reconciliation is an opportunity for you and God to work together to form the-best-version-of-yourself.

Common Objections

There are of course some common objections to the sacrament of Reconciliation.

The secular culture propagates the myth that there is no such thing as sin and that we never were sinners. They tell us that these are just ideas the Church invented to control and manipulate us. I assure you, sin and evil are real. This truth should require no proof or explanation. If you feel it does, turn on your television this evening and watch the news, or take a casual walk through world history.

This secular view seems almost absurd the moment it is removed from the self-centered, pleasure-seeking environment that keeps it alive. The non-Catholic Christian objections to the sacrament of Reconciliation, however, require considerably more discernment.

The catch-cry of modern Christians has become, "I don't need to confess my sins to a priest, I can confess them straight to God." You can do anything you want; that is the nature of the freedom with which God endows us. But if you are serious about being

Christian, then it follows that you are serious about doing the will of God.

Is it not the Protestants and Evangelicals who claim to have such a firm grip on the Bible?

The tradition of Reconcilation is deeply rooted in the life and teachings of Jesus, as evidenced in the Gospels. I have often wondered how non-Catholic Christians are able to ignore or explain away some of these central passages. For example, what is to be said of John's account of Pentecost, "'Peace be with you. As the Father has sent me, so I am sending you.' And when he had said this, he breathed on them and said, 'Receive the Holy Spirit. Whose sins you forgive are forgiven them, and whose sins you retain are retained'" (John 20:21-23).

Today, many Catholics subscribe to this Protestant-Evangelical view, and sadly, their position has been forged not only by Protestant-Evangelical propaganda, but also by the writings of some Catholic theologians of the late twentieth century.

The objection has been raised that Reconciliation (or Confession as it was known as until the late 1900s) was only instituted in 1215 at the Fourth Lateran Council, and therefore was not part of Christian tradition from the beginning. This is clearly not the case. While the earliest Christian writings such as *Didache* from the first century are not clear on the form or procedure to be used for the forgiveness of sins, Irenaeus makes it clear in his writings that the sacrament goes back to the beginning of the Church. Christian writers of the third and fourth centuries such as Origen, Cyprian, and Aphraates also make it clear that Confession is to be made to a priest, and we have no reason to believe that this was not the practice from the beginning. Writing around 244, Origen refers to the sinner who "does not shrink from declaring his sin to a priest of the Lord" (*In Leviticum Homiliae*). Seven years later, Cyprian writes, "Finally, of how much greater faith and more salutary fear are they who... confess to the priests of God in a straightforward manner and in sorrow, making an open declaration of their conscience" (*De Lapsis*). Writing to advise priests, Aphraates says, "If anyone uncovers his wound before you, give him the remedy of repentance. And he that is ashamed to make known his weakness, encourage him so that he will not hide it from you. And when he has revealed it to you, do not make it public" (*Demonstrationes*).

The Fourth Lateran Council didn't invent the practice of Confession or Reconciliation, as we know it today. The Council sought only to reaffirm what had been the constant practice of Christians since the beginning, and emphasize the advantages of this practice for all men and women who desire to draw nearer to God.

—◦◦◦—

Among those Catholics who still hold a place for Reconciliation in their spiritual life, there is yet another faction who believe it is necessary only in the case of mortal sin. This argument makes me wonder what type of relationships these people have with their spouses, employers, and close friends.

Let us take as our example a relationship between a husband and a wife. Would it be good for their marriage if they never apologized to each other for anything? In 1970, the movie *Love Story* was a huge hit and went on to win an Academy Award and three Golden Globes. The most famous line from the movie proclaims, "Love means never having to say you're sorry." I wonder what impact that one line has had on viewers' relationships with the people they love and their relationships with God. The screenwriter has clearly confused love with pride.

Would it be healthy for a relationship if a husband and wife apologized only for mortal offenses? How healthy would the key relationships in your life be if these were the guidelines? I would suggest that they would not be healthy at all; rather, they would be massively dysfunctional and woefully inadequate. If we continue to apply these guidelines to our relationship with God, our relationship with God will suffer the fate that so many modern human relationships are suffering.

—✧—

These represent the common objections that the people of our present age have toward the sacrament of Reconciliation. But with all that said, I would like to affirm once more that God is not an unjust dictator trying to rule humanity with an iron fist. God doesn't want to control or manipulate you; he doesn't want to force you to do things you don't want to do; and he doesn't want to make you feel guilty and bad about yourself. God wants you to become the-best-version-of-yourself. Prayer, the sacraments, and the Scriptures are all wonderful gifts designed to help us resolve our inner tensions so we can make the journey.

Behold the Beauty

We all have spiritual disease. We all have sins. Some people like to pretend that they don't, but their sins will just spread through their lives like cancer in the body. And in the end, they will be devoured by their sins. Other people try to justify their sins with all types of explanations, none of which will ever satisfy their own hearts. There are those who go to experts with the hope that such people will help them overcome their troubled consciences.

If you want to spend the rest of your life arguing for your weaknesses, so be it. If you want to tell yourself, "it's my character," go ahead. If you want to have someone try to explain away or justify your sins, go to a psychologist or a psychiatrist. But if you want peace in your heart, come to Reconciliation. If you want the joy of a clear conscience, come to Reconciliation.

The mysteries of grace can never be adequately described in cold words on cold pages. They must be experienced. So if you haven't been to Reconciliation for a while, maybe now is your time. Perhaps it has been ten years, or twenty years, maybe even longer. "Do not be afraid" (Matthew 14:27). Bring the sins of your life, and place them at the feet of a priest who, in the sacrament of Reconciliation, sits in for Jesus. Do not think of it as confessing your sins to a priest. Think of it as confessing your sins to Christ alive in that priest.

God sees your unrealized potential. He sees not only who you are, but also who you can be. Ask him to share that vision with you.

A great freedom is born by bringing our darkness into the light. Our faults and failings have a tendency of eating away at us inside. But when we bring them into the light they lose their power over us.

I assure you, if you will approach this sacrament with a sincere and humble heart, you will experience the flow of grace in your life. Listen to those words of absolution: "By the ministry of the Church, may God grant you pardon and peace, and I absolve you from your sins in the name of the Father, and of the Son, and of the Holy Spirit." And as the priest speaks these words, the floodgates of grace will be opened, your soul will be filled with a deep peace, and you will experience an inexplicable lightness, a sense of liberation.

Reconciliation is a gift. Behold the beauty. Embrace the treasure.

Self-Knowledge

In the spiritual life, it is very important not only to grow in our knowledge and understanding of God, but also in our knowledge and understanding of ourselves. Both knowledge of God and knowledge of self are necessary to make the Journey of the Soul. These two are inextricably linked. And one without the other is useless.

Confessing our sins in the sacrament of Reconciliation helps us to develop this self-knowledge. The saints had this self-knowledge. They developed it from hours of self-examination and a consistent practice of Reconciliation. They knew their strengths and weaknesses, their faults, failings, flaws, and defects, their talents and abilities, their needs and desires, their hopes and their dreams, their potential and their purpose.

They were not afraid to look at themselves as they really were by the light of God's grace in prayer. They knew that the things of this world are passing, and that when this brief life is over, we will each stand naked in the presence of God. At that moment, money, power, status, possessions, and worldly fame will mean nothing. The only thing that has value in that moment is character - the light within you. Who we become is infinitely more important than what we do or what we have. Or as Francis once said, "Remember, you are what you are in the eyes of God, and nothing else."

Get to know yourself. The gifts of self-knowledge include freedom from the world's image of you and compassion for others. The more I get to know myself and my own brokenness, the more I am able to accept and love others. Furthermore, the more I get to know myself, the more I am able to understand others and be tolerant of their faults, failings, flaws, addictions, and brokenness. Self-knowledge breeds the ultimate form of compassion.

Get to know yourself, and every relationship in your life will improve.

A New Habit

I am convinced that our lives change when our habits change, and I have been convinced of the power of regular Reconciliation in my own life. So I would like to encourage you to make Reconciliation a spiritual habit in your life.

A couple of weeks ago, I heard a friend speak about it in relation to washing his car. He explained it in this way: If you wash your car every couple of weeks, you tend to take very good care of it. You don't throw food around in it, and if you see a puddle of mud in the road you go around it. But after a few weeks without a wash, it gets messy on the inside and dirty on the outside, and you become less careful with it. You just throw another piece of trash in the back seat because there is already so much that you won't notice the extra piece.

Your soul is the same. You go to Reconciliation and it becomes clean and sparkling. But after a few weeks, the little sins begin to pile up, and before you know it, a big sin doesn't look so bad on top of a pile of small sins. And once you add the big one to the pile, you figure you've made a mess already so you might as well really make a mess. Little by little, you begin to lose your sense of sin. Before you know it, you are very unhappy, and you don't really know why. You begin to experience a certain restlessness and an anxiety, but you don't know what is causing it.

No one can tell you how often you should go to Reconciliation. The Church requires that you go at least once a year, but encourages regular confession. Some people go once a week, others go once a month, and there has long been a rumor that the present Holy Father confesses everyday.

My experience has been that once a month is a good thing. If you haven't been in a while, at first you may wish to go every week to redevelop your spiritual senses. This weekly Reconciliation may be particularly helpful if you are caught in some habitual sins. But as the weeks pass, most people should be able to apply the rhythm of monthly Reconciliation to their spiritual life.

Temptation

Once we have turned back to God and embraced him again like the prodigal son embraced his father (cf. Luke 15:20), we must then return to the world. Here we must face all the distractions and temptations that drew us away from the path of peace before.

I know only one immutable truth when it comes to the struggle with temptation: Don't dialogue with the tempter.

When he whispers in your ear, turn away from him. He will say things like, "everybody is doing it" or "it won't matter just this once" or "Nobody will know." Don't surrender the peace in your soul. The temptation will pass. The best way to pass the time while you are waiting for temptation to pass is to pray. Replace the dialogue of temptation with a dialogue of prayer. "God, I know what is good and true, but I am still attracted to what is self-destructive. Give me strength. Be my strength." Sometimes the temptation is so great that you are not even able to formulate your own words in your head. It is then that you will learn the values of those simple prayers that the modern world despises so much: "Our Father, who art in heaven…" (Matthew 6:9), or "Hail Mary, Full of Grace…" (Luke 1:28).

Whatever you do, don't dialogue with the devil. He always has more questions than you have answers. He will suggest one thing, and you will reply in thought with a rebuttal. But the back and forth will wear you out. Eventually you will give into the sin out of sheer exhaustion or just to end the dialogue. Sin is exhausting. Avoid the dialogue that precedes sin. Temptation is real. Get to know how it takes place in your life, and avoid those situations where you know you will be tempted.

When the tempter whispers in your ear, turn your back on him. Why complicate your life? Turn to God and pray. Don't dialogue with the tempter.

———

To know your strengths and weaknesses is a great advantage in any field. In the spiritual realm, it is of ultimate importance. The proud basketball player doesn't notice the faults in his game. The proud businesswoman doesn't notice the weaknesses in her business. A proud artist doesn't notice the defect in her style. The proud man doesn't notice the weakness in his character.

The proud must content themselves with mediocrity. Excellence belongs to the humble.

The Touch of the Master's Hand

In her wisdom, my fourth grade teacher, Mrs. Rutter, introduced my classmates to the following poem. After reciting it one day, she announced that over the next week, we were all to learn the poem by heart. Then everyday for about a month someone would recite the poem for the class. It was just one example of her many moments of genius. At the time, our understanding of it was shallow, perhaps because one must experience some of the hard knocks of life to truly appreciate the full meaning. The piece is entitled "The Touch of the Master's Hand," by Myra B. Welch.

Amazing things are possible if we allow the Master to lay his hands on our lives.

—*∿∿*—

'Twas battered and scarred, and the auctioneer
Thought it scarcely worth his while
To waste much time on the old violin,
But held it up with a smile.
"What am I bidden, good folks," he cried,
"Who'll start the bidding for me?"
"A dollar, a dollar," then, two! Only two?
"Two dollars, and who'll make it three?
"Three dollars, once; three dollars twice;
Going for three..." But no,
From the room, far back, a grey haired man
Came forward and picked up the bow;
Then, wiping the dust from the old violin,
And tightening the loose strings,
He played a melody pure and sweet

As a caroling angel sings.
The music ceased, and the auctioneer,
With a voice that was quiet and low,
Said, "What am I bid for the old violin?"
And held it up with the bow.
"A thousand dollars, and who'll make it two?
Two thousand! And who'll make it three?
Three thousand, once; three thousand twice;
And going and gone," said he.
The people cheered, but some of them cried,
"We do not quite understand
What changed its worth?" Swift came the reply:
"The touch of a master's hand."

And many a man with life out of tune,
And battered and scarred with sin,
Is auctioned cheap to the thoughtless crowd
Much like the old violin.
A "mess of potage," a glass of wine;
A game – and he travels on.
He is "going" once, and "going" twice,
He's "going" and almost "gone."
But the Master comes and the foolish crowd
Never can quite understand
The worth of a soul
    and the change that's wrought
By the touch of the master's hand.

CHAPTER THIRTEEN

CONTEMPLATION

We all live lives of contemplation. The question is, What do *you* contemplate? Is it the riches of the world? Is it every woman that passes you in the street? Is it fame? Power? Or, do you contemplate the wonders of God, the glory of his creation, and the joys of the spiritual life?

It is not necessary to go away to a monastery to live a life of contemplation. We are all contemplatives. And what you contemplate will play a very significant role in the life you live.

Osmosis

We live in a time of tremendous cultural pressure. "The spirit of the world" is strong, and there is little support for those who choose to reject "the spirit of the world" and embrace "the Spirit of God." This is not a popular choice, and as a result, can often create a certain loneliness in our lives.

Osmosis is the scientific theory that states, what is more dense will filter through to what is less dense. If we are going to be true to our values and become the-best-version-of-ourselves, we need to build up a certain density within us. This inner strength, or density, will allow us to resist the pressure to abandon our values and our true selves.

When we have this density within us, we will have a Christian effect on our environment. When we don't have this density, our environment will affect us. What is more dense filters through to what is less dense.

The most powerful way to build this density, this inner strength, is prayer.

Thought Determines Action

The actions of your life are determined by your last most dominant thought.

For a moment, imagine you are a basketball player. It's game seven in the playoffs for the NBA championship. There is one second left on the clock. The scores are tied. You have just been fouled, and you have one shot.

Between the time the foul is called and the time you shoot the ball, everything moves in slow motion. There are one hundred million people watching you, but really all there is, is you and your thoughts. If, during those moments, you imagine yourself missing the shot, what will happen? Exactly. You'll miss the shot. If you imagine yourself making the shot, what will happen? Of course, you will make it. What if you imagine yourself missing the shot 47 times and making the shot 23 times, what will happen then? You'll miss it. Why? Because the actions of your life are determined by your last most *dominant* thought.

To be Catholic means to be striving to become more like Jesus. If we are serious about being Catholic, we must then place our attention on Jesus and the ways we can apply his teachings to modern living.

When I was in high school, we went away on retreat. At that time, I was fairly disinterested in things of a spiritual nature, yet I seem to remember vaguely that the theme of the retreat was placing Christ at the center of our lives. Over and over for three days, the speakers spoke about living a "Christ-centered" life.

Over the past ten years, I have discovered that this is not just a nice phrase or idea, but that it is, in fact, the very core of Catholic spirituality. The centrality of Christ in human history and in our individual lives is no small discovery. Furthermore, the centrality of Christ in each human life is not just an idea. It is an idea that has been tried and tested, and the results are awe-inspiring.

Have you ever wondered how the saints became so focused in their practice of virtue? Earlier we said that the difference between the saints and those who have been less successful in living the values of Christianity was that the saints affixed their singleness of purpose to the great Spiritual North Star. Furthermore, we established that they had better habits. These habits were not only external habits, but also internal habits.

One such habit was the way they pondered the Gospels. In every waking moment of every hour of every day, they were contemplating the life and teachings of Jesus Christ.

Thought determines action. Before too long, you will be living out what has already happened in your mind. The actions of your life are determined by your last most dominant thought. Human thought is creative. What we think becomes. What you allow to occupy your mind forms the reality of your life. Good or bad, everything happens in your mind before it happens in time and space. If you can direct what happens in your mind, you can direct what happens in your life.

What are you thinking? What do you think about all day long? What do you think about in the car on the way to and from work each day? What do you think about while you are waiting in line at the supermarket?

I know this for certain: whatever you place your attention on will increase in your life. If you place your attention on money, you will have more money. If you place your attention on power, you will have more power. And if you place your attention on virtue, you will have more virtue.

Paul gives us this advice: "Whatever is true, whatever is honorable, whatever is just, whatever is pure, whatever is lovely, whatever is gracious, if there is any excellence, if there is anything worthy of praise, think about these things" (Philippians 4:8).

You cannot grow an oak tree with an apple seed. So it is with thoughts. Certain thoughts give birth to certain actions.

The Classroom of Silence

If I asked you to go out and find some suitable candidates to be prophets and leaders in the modern world, where would you look? Would you ask yourself, where can I find myself some shepherds? The most common profession amongst the prophets and leaders of the Old Testament was shepherding. Why do you suppose God called so many shepherds to occupy positions of authority and influence? Perhaps it was because they were out in the middle of God's cosmic temple all day, and in the middle of God's cosmic Classroom of Silence they had plenty of time to think, reflect, ponder, and listen to the voice of God in their lives.

If I live to be a hundred and speak and write for my whole life, I will never be able to emphasize enough how important silence is as an ingredient of the spiritual life. In *A Call to Joy* I wrote, "You will learn more from an hour of silence than you can in a year from books." In *Mustard Seeds* I wrote, "It is in the Classroom of Silence that God bestows his wisdom on men and women."

I will make two promises to you. In the silence, you will find God. In the silence, you will find yourself. These will be the two greatest discoveries of your life. But, these discoveries will not be epiphany-type moments. They will be gradual. You will discover a little at a time, something like a jigsaw puzzle being put together. Without these discoveries, I cannot imagine how incomplete and miserable life would be. It is this process of discovery that makes sense of life.

Our modern world is spinning out of control, and one of the chief contributors to the chaos and confusion of our modern age is noise. Our lives are filled with noise. We are afraid of silence.

During the 1940s, C.S. Lewis wrote a series of letters, which appeared in The Guardian. These letters were the correspondence between a senior devil, Screwtape, and an apprentice devil, his nephew Wormwood. The thirty-one letters were later published in the form of a book entitled The Screwtape Letters. In the letters, Screwtape is advising Wormwood about the procedure for winning a soul away from God and toward hell both on earth and in eternity. At one point, Wormwood is trying to think up all types of exotic ways to tempt the man who has been assigned to him, and Screwtape rebukes him, explaining that their methods have long been established. One such method, he explains, is to create so much noise in the life of man that he can no longer hear the voice of God. In one letter, the senior devil Screwtape announces, "We will make the whole universe a noise in the end."

I believe the writings of C.S. Lewis were operating in a prophetic capacity when he expressed this idea more than fifty years ago.

Today, we wake up to clock radios, we listen to the radio while we shower, and we watch television while we eat breakfast. We listen to the radio in the car on the way to work or school, we listen to music all day over the intercom, we get put on hold and we listen to the radio. We have Gameboys, pagers, cell phones, Walkmans, Discmans, even DVD-mans. Most homes have multiple televisions, and we leave them on even when nobody is watching them...

Our world has been filled with noise, and as a result, we can no longer hear the voice of God in our lives.

A Starting Point

The two things lacking in most people's lives are intimacy with God and intimacy with self. Most people don't know who they are or why they are here. Most people feel far from God. And most people think that these gaps are too wide to bridge.

This lack of intimacy with God and self limits any possible intimacy with others.

As many of you are aware from my talks and previous writings, the adventure of salvation began for me when I started spending ten minutes a day in a quiet church on my way to college each morning. It is here, in these moments of silence, that I first began to consciously develop an awareness of self and God. It was here, in the Classroom of Silence, that I came to realize that God is only as far away as we place him.

Ten minutes a day. If you are confused, angry, tired, frustrated, happy, excited, grateful... whatever, come to the silence. Stick a note on your bathroom mirror. TEN MINUTES A DAY. And everyday as you brush your teeth, ask yourself, "When will I spend my ten minutes in the Classroom of Silence today?" Don't be deceived by the simplicity of this message. You will be amazed how much ten minutes each day in a quiet church can change your life.

My staff estimate almost two million people have heard this message in the last seven years. Some nights after my talks, I lay awake in bed wondering how many made the effort to stick that note on their mirror. I know the overwhelming majority didn't, but that doesn't bother me. I fall asleep contented, because I know the lives of those who did stick that note on their mirrors are about to change forever. I know they will begin to feel the joy that God has so graciously allowed me to experience.

Wouldn't it be nice if our souls growled when they were hungry, like our stomachs do? Your immortal soul is the most valuable possession you have. The saints knew this, and they protected it and nourished it and nurtured it. I hope one day soon, you will realize this too, not in your mind, but in your heart. And having come to this realization, I hope you will begin to nourish and nurture your soul. Only then will you truly thrive.

———

Beyond the power of silence in the lives of individuals, I can attest to the power of silence in a community. There is a phenomenon sweeping the Catholic world. It is known as Eucharistic Adoration. It may be considered old-fashioned and overly pious by some, but I assure you, wherever you find Eucharistic Adoration in a parish, those communities are thriving. The people are more spiritually focused, more involved, these communities are more vibrant, and vocations are abundant in these parishes.

When are we finally going to stop casting these signs aside as if they were merely coincidence?

While modern man is filling his life with more and more noise and trying to absent God from more and more areas of his life, God is inviting us into the silence and into his presence.

Here in this "sacrament of love," we will find rest for our weary hearts and minds. In the great Classroom of Silence and in the presence of our God, we will develop resolute hearts and peaceful spirits. I can hear Jesus calling to us with a clarity that is unmistakable, "Come to me all you who labor and are heavy laden, and I will give you rest" (Matthew 11:28).

Come into the silence.

The Big Question

If we wish to encourage today's saints to emerge, we must simply return one question to our inner dialogue. I call it The Big Question. As far as I can see, it is the ultimate question, the only question.

"God, what do you think I should do?"

To think that we can find happiness in our lives without asking this question makes us the king or queen of fantasyland.

We make decisions everyday. Some of them are large and most of them are small. But, when was the last time you sat down with the Divine Architect and asked, "God, what do you think I should do in this situation with my spouse?" When was the last time you sat down with the Divine Navigator and asked, "God, what do you think I should do in this situation with my children?" When your kids come to you to talk about what they are thinking of doing with their lives, do you just ask them what they want to do? Or do you ask them what they feel God is calling them to?

I've seen happy people and I've seen miserable people, and I can tell you without any shadow of a doubt, the difference between the truly happy people in this world and the miserable people is one thing: a sense of mission.

People who are passionate, energetic, and enthusiastic about life have a sense of mission in their lives. They are not living their lives in the selfish pursuit of pleasure or possessions. They are living out a mission, and through that mission, they are making a difference in other people's lives.

What's your mission?

How will you discover your mission?

Perhaps the first realization is you don't choose a mission. Someone sends you on a mission.

—⟊⟊⟊—

"Most men lead lives of quiet desperation." If you don't ask The Big Question, you will not discover your mission, and sooner or later you will be numbered amongst Thoreau's masses. You won't aim to, or plan to live a life of quiet desperation; you'll just wake up one morning and wonder how you got there.

If you are already living a life of quiet desperation, you don't have to stay there. Just start asking The Big Question. "God, what do you think I should do?" Make it a constant part of your inner dialogue, and I promise you, your life will start to change.

—⁓—

Life is vocational. Each of us is created for a reason. With the shortage of vocations to the priesthood and religious life, we have forgotten that marriage and the single life are also worthy vocations. And because of our inability to reconcile sexual intimacy and holiness, the nobility of marriage as a vocation is often undermined. All this confusion leaves many people thinking that some people have a vocation and others don't. Everyone has a vocation, and unveiling that vocation is critically important to our experience of life. Life is vocational.

I guess it all comes down to deciding how long you want to be happy. If you just want moments of happiness, I suspect pleasure and possessions can satisfy. If you want to be happy for an hour, take a nap. If you want to be happy for a whole day, go shopping. If you want to be happy for weekend, go fishing. If you want to be happy for a month, take a trip to Australia. If you want to be happy for a whole year, inherit a fortune. But if you want to be happy for a lifetime, find a way to make a difference in other people's lives.

Action without Prayer

Action without prayer is the curse of most modern humanitarian organizations, and sadly, it is a pitfall into which many local church groups have also fallen.

When we become preoccupied with action and neglect prayer, this social activism reduces the Church to little more than a social welfare committee. Action without prayer is useless.

There is a great danger to action without prayer. Don't we tell our children, "Think before you act?" Thought is to the natural realm what prayer is to the supernatural realm.

Before you rush off and start building a new life for yourself, make sure you are building what the Divine Architect has envisioned. Don't just go off and start building – pray, and allow him to guide you.

Geography of Prayer

When I was a child, my prayer was completely focused on myself and what I wanted. I prayed to score a goal at soccer, I prayed to do well in my exams, and I prayed that the girl in math class would like me. The geography of my prayer was confined to my physical location. Life in a loving environment draws us out of our selfishness, and as I grew older, I began to pray for my family, my neighbors, and my friends. Gradually, the geography of my prayer began to expand. At different times, when there were floods or fires in Australia, I would pray for the people in those places. When I was twenty, I began to travel the world. It was only then that the geography of my prayer really began to expand. Everyday, I was encountering people who were out of work, people struggling with addictions, men and women tormented by divorce, people wrestling with depression, and in many places the hungry and the homeless.

Today, most of my work is in America. Each day, I choose a state, and I offer my trials and sufferings of that day for the people of that state. I pray that the people in that state who read my books and hear my talks will open their hearts to the message.

What's the geography of your prayer?

Begin Today

Perhaps your last concern is that you don't know how to pray. It is much simpler than you suppose. Step into the silence, and in your heart, say to God, "I do not know how to pray." Already you will have begun to pray. Speak to him. Simply open your heart to him in a gentle dialogue. Just talk to him.

When you leave your time of prayer, continue the dialogue with God in your heart in the moments of your day. Share with him your joys and your disappointments, your questions and your doubts. Speak with him about everything.

Tevye, from Fiddler on the Roof, is a great example. He is always talking to God... about everything. This constant dialogue is perhaps part of what Paul had in mind when he wrote, "Pray constantly" (1 Thessalonians 5:17).

—⟶⟶—

In the final analysis, the measure of your life will be the measure of your prayer. Action without prayer is useless. Action that springs forth from prayer is the work of God.

CHAPTER FOURTEEN

MASS

At the center of the Catholic tradition is the Mass. It is in the Mass that the 1.2 billion Catholics around the world come together to share a common experience. But the wisdom of regular worship has a much deeper meaning than bringing us all together once a week; it is a profound reflection of God's blueprint for all of creation.

I wrote *The Rhythm of Life* not only for a Catholic audience, nor alone for a Christian audience, but for the whole cross section of society. And yet, I learned the premise upon which I based the book from the way the Church structures our practice of Christianity. Everything in creation has rhythm. Rhythm is at the core of God's genius for creation. As man turns to God, he is invited to use this same blueprint for his life. In

Genesis, we read that God created the world in six days and rested on the seventh. He didn't rest because he was tired. God rested on the seventh day because he foresaw our need for rest.

The seasons change to a rhythm. The tides come in and go out to a rhythm. The sun rises and sets to a rhythm. Your heart pumps blood through your body to a rhythm. Plants grow according to the process of photosynthesis, which is based on a rhythm. And ultimately, the workings of a woman's body are based on a rhythm - and that rhythm gives forth new life. The rhythm gives birth to harmony, efficiency, effectiveness, health, happiness, peace, and prosperity. Destroy the rhythm, and you invite chaos, confusion, destruction, and disorder.

This is the wisdom upon which the Church bases our worship as Catholics. The Church bases the calendar on the rhythm that God has placed at the center of creation. In turn, the Church hopes this will help us to place this essential rhythm at the center of our own lives.

It is within this context that we can begin to understand Sunday as a day of rest and renewal, and more specifically, the role of the Mass in the Catholic lifestyle.

Rediscovering the Mass

Just like in the time of Francis, for many modern Catholics Mass has become more of a habit and a social gathering than an expression of genuine conviction.

On my way to Mass this morning, it occurred to me that if Muslims believed that God was truly present in their mosques, and that by some mystical power they could receive and consume him in the form of bread and wine, they would crawl over red-hot broken glass for the chance. But as Catholics, we are so unaware of the mystery and the privilege that we can hardly wait to get out of church.

Over and over, you and I have heard people complain about the Mass. Perhaps at different times we have even been the person complaining. "Mass is boring." "The music is too old-fashioned." "The music is too modern." "I couldn't understand what the priest was trying to say." "The sound system is no good." "I cannot relate to the priest." "The people at Mass are not my age."

Maybe, just maybe, we are missing the point.

The way I see it is, we've lost our sense of wonder. It is true for almost every area of our lives, but particularly when it comes to matters of faith and spirituality. We have lost the quintessential quality of childhood – wonder.

Do you experience the wonder? Do you sense the mystery and power of receiving and consuming your God in the Eucharist? Do you marvel at the fact? If we do believe that Christ is truly present in the Eucharist, then the power unleashed within us by the consumption of the Eucharist is unfathomable.

I often wonder as I watch great athletes compete, knowing that they are not Catholic, how much better they would perform if they believed Christ was present in the Eucharist and that they could receive him before a race. And what is true for these athletes is also true for our lives. There is great power in the Eucharist.

We don't go to Mass to socialize. We don't go to be entertained. We go to receive. We go to Mass to be fed and nourished by the Word of God – both in Scripture and in Sacrament. Open your heart, open your mind, and open your spirit.

Life is not about what sort of shoes you wear. It's not about what street you live on. It is not about how much money you have in the bank or what sort of car you drive. It's not about whether or not you get that promotion, or where you and your family vacation each year. Life is not about who you have dated, who you are dating, or who you married. It is not about whether you made the football team. Life is not about what college you went to, what college may or may not accept you, or what college your children are going to. Life isn't about these things.

Life is about who you love and who you hurt. Life is about how you love yourself and how you hurt yourself. It's about how you love and hurt the people in your life. You can't see these things, but they are powerful and real.

Mass is not about who you sit next to. It's not about which priest says Mass. It is not about what you wear or who is there. Mass is not about the music. It's not even about the preaching. Mass is about receiving the body and blood of Christ, not just physically, but spiritually. Perhaps you have been receiving the Eucharist physically every Sunday for your whole life. Next Sunday, prepare yourself, be conscious of the marvel, the wonder, the mystery, and receive spiritually.

Rediscover the wonder.

A Personal Prayer

Each Sunday as I walk into Church, I make one small request of God: "Lord, show me one way I can become a better person this week."

He never fails me.

Sometimes he shows me in a song and sometimes in the Scriptures. Sometimes he answers me through the person sitting next to me, and sometimes with something the priest says.

Like every activity in our lives, the Mass can be understood and appreciated only in the context of the journey we are making. It is only in this context that we can learn to truly value the Mass as an extraordinary gift.

It has been my experience that simple and practical resolutions change our lives. So I will offer you one.

Go out and buy yourself a new writing journal some time this week. Next Sunday, as you go into Church, ask God, "Lord, show me one way I can become a better person this week." When you get home, take a page and write that one point God revealed to you in the journal. Each day, when you take your ten minutes in the Classroom of Silence, use this one thought as your starting point. Talk to God about how you can apply it to your life.

As the weeks pass, you will have more and more inspirations to use in your time of prayer. After a year, you will be able to pass through the pages and see how far you have come.

Our lives change when our habits change. They don't have to be enormous new habits. Small, simple, practical resolutions will suffice.

The Prayers of the Mass

The prayers of the Mass remind us of the Journey of the Soul and orient us toward the great Spiritual North Star. There is great beauty in these prayers, but too often we don't hear them because we are distracted by our thoughts or by those around us. Some of the prayers in the Mass are the same every time we go. Others change with the seasons of the Church calendar. And some still, change everyday. If you take time to listen and truly pray these prayers as the priest does, you will discover the intimate knowledge the Church has of the people's spiritual needs.

I would be the first to admit that it is difficult to concentrate on these prayers during the Mass sometimes. For that reason, I would really like to encourage you to get yourself a missal. I know... it's a little old-fashioned, but owning a missal took my understanding and appreciation of the Mass to a whole new level.

A couple of months after I started spending ten minutes a day in my local church each morning, I began attending Mass in the parish on Tuesday evenings, and a month or so later on Friday mornings also. It was at Mass during the week that my love for this sacred ritual really began to be ignited. I would follow the opening and closing prayers, as well as the readings in my missal, and the words began to probe my heart and enflame the fire in my soul.

The prayers of the Mass are beautifully integrated and carefully designed to keep our focus on the great Spiritual North Star. For example, the opening prayer on the Twenty-First Week of Ordinary Time is, "Father, help us to seek the values that will bring us lasting joy in this changing world. In our desire for what you promise, make us one in mind and heart." The opening prayers of the Mass guide us to focus on the themes that will emerge in the readings that day. This is the opening prayer for Friday during the Fourth Week of Lent: "Father, our source of life, you know our weakness. May we reach out with joy to grasp your hand and walk more readily in your ways."

Get yourself a missal and just follow the opening prayer, the readings, and the closing prayer, and your experience in Mass will increase exponentially. Then during the week, make a habit of going to Mass one day or two days. This more intimate experience of the sacrament will truly fan the fire of your soul. On the other days when you don't attend Mass, use the prayers and the readings of the day from the missal during your time of prayer.

Our lives change when our habits change. The only way for the Church to become more spiritual is for the people to be become more spiritual. We become more spiritual when we pursue spiritual habits. This is one real and practical way to unearth the riches of Catholicism in our day-to-day lives.

My Favorite Prayer

Do you have a favorite part of the Mass? I do. Mine is right before the sign of peace, when the priest prays, "Deliver us, Lord, from every evil, and grant us peace in our day. In your mercy keep us free from sin and protect us from all anxiety as we wait in joyful hope for the coming of our Savior, Jesus Christ."

These words mean so much to me. To live a life free from sin is a simple desire, but a noble one. There is an Australian song entitled "Tenterfield Saddler" that was part of my childhood. It's about a man named George who lived in a small country town. All day long he would sit on his verandah making horse saddles, and over the years he became a sage-like figure for the locals. The song begins,

> The late George Woolnogh
> Worked on High Street
> Lived on manners
> For 52 years he sat on his verandah
> And made his saddles.
>
> And if you had questions
> About sheep or flowers or dogs
> You just asked the saddler
> He lived without sin
> They're building a library for him.

—∿∿—

I have seen how sin complicates our lives, confuses our minds, and hardens our hearts. I have seen the devastating effects of sin in my own life, in the lives of the people I love, and in the lives of complete strangers. I want to live a life free from sin, and the prayer "keep us free from sin" resonates with the deepest desires of my heart. I love the peace that is the fruit of a clear conscience.

"Protect us from all anxiety." How much of our lives do we waste worrying? A friend of mine has a quote on her answering machine that says, "Worry doesn't empty tomorrow of its suffering, it empties today of its strength."

I know it is the sin in my life that causes my pain, anguish, impatience, anxiety, and restlessness. We waste so much time and energy on sin.

Imagine how much you and I could accomplish if we didn't waste so much time and energy on sin!

Our Father

A good friend of mine volunteers in Chicago prisons, visiting the prisoners and leading Bible studies. Not too long ago, he invited me to visit a maximum-security facility and speak to the prisoners. I accepted the invitation, and a couple of weeks before the event was scheduled to take place, I asked to speak with the three chaplains from the prison to get a sense of the group. They told me many things about the group, but the most alarming fact they shared was in relation to the entire male prison population in America. Statistically, it has been shown that ninety percent of male prisoners in America today between the ages of 16 and 30 grew up separated from their biological fathers. Ninety percent!

I believe the present fatherless generation is the result of the evil forces that tempt our hearts. You may not be separated from your biological father, but these same evil forces want to sow in you the seeds of doubt, skepticism, and cynicism. And in doing so, they separate you from your heavenly Father.

The devil wants to orphan you. He wants to drag you away from your Father. He wants to steal from you the Spirit that leads you to cry out to God, "Abba Father." He wants to kidnap you away from your spiritual Father. He wants to distract you from the gentle and persistent call of your heavenly Father. Don't let him. Ponder just those first two words of this ancient prayer – "Our Father." If we could really understand this single truth of God as Father, we would weep for joy every time this prayer crossed our lips.

I also believe that the liberty and equality that men and women have struggled with and searched for throughout history have been revealed through this simple prayer. If only we could understand and grasp the fact that we are all children of God. Only then will we relate to each other as we should.

Offering

I have also observed that the time surrounding the offertory and collection seems to have been unofficially declared, by the power of common practice, the time to look around and see who is in church, to ascertain what everyone is wearing, and to tell whoever you are with something you forgot to tell them prior to Mass.

Contrary to this popular practice, this time is actually designed for a very important spiritual practice. On the altar, the priest is preparing the gifts to be offered. While the priest is offering the gifts, the appropriate disposition of heart, mind, and spirit would be to unite ourselves with the gifts on the altar. Place yourself on the altar. Unite yourself with the offering of the bread and wine about to be transformed into the body and blood of Christ. Perhaps then, a transformation similar to that, which is brought upon the gifts by consecration, will be brought upon you and your life.

The Mass is supposed to unite us with and transform us in Christ.

If you want to know what is keeping you from growing closer to God and becoming the-best-version-of-yourself, bring everything to God. Mentally, place everything on the altar before God. Your worries, your hopes, your dreams. Your faults, your failings, your sins. Your ambitions, your potential, your talents. Your possessions, your career, your money.

Whatever you are not able to place on the altar is what is holding you back.

Embrace the Gift

God doesn't call us to church on Sunday because he has some egotistical need for us all to fall down before him and worship him at ten o'clock every Sunday morning. It isn't designed to help him; it's designed to help us. It isn't intended to make him happy; it's intended to allow us to share in his happiness.

The Mass is filled with riches. It is an unfathomable gift. Embrace the gift.

CHAPTER FIFTEEN

THE BIBLE

Of all the books ever written or published, the Bible is the most widely read, studied, translated, distributed, and quoted. It is the best selling book of all times. When it comes to learning about the nature of God and his desires for us, no other book comes close. In the Bible, we discover the depth and generosity of God's love, as well as his desire to soothe humanity's yearning for truth and happiness. Where did the Bible come from? How did we come to be blessed with such a rare treasure?

Where Did the Bible Come From?

I begin our discussion of the Scriptures with these questions because, in recent Christian history, the Bible has been kidnapped by Protestants and Evangelicals.

At one time or another, most Catholics have been cornered by an over zealous Christian in the workplace or supermarket. They immediately start quoting Scripture, and oftentimes their well argued ideas leave us tired, confused, filled with doubts, and feeling spiritually inadequate. Chances are, if the conversation proceeds to any length, they will approach the idea that the Bible is the one and only source of inspiration, direction, and revelation. This of course is an attack upon the Catholic Church, however carefully masked or subtly presented; for as Catholics, we believe that both the "Sacred Scriptures and sacred Tradition form one sacred deposit of the word of God" (Dei Verbum). God reveals himself in nature, God reveals himself in the Scriptures, and God reveals himself in the life of the Church.

It is the dynamic interaction between the Scriptures and Tradition that keeps the Word alive. If you separate the Scriptures from the living, breathing institution they were entrusted to, they lose their life. This of course is a major point of contention between Catholics and other non-Catholic Christians. But, with this background and as an attempt to shed a little light on this point of contention, let us return to the original question. Where did the Bible come from?

Well, it didn't just drop down from Heaven one fine day, nor did it appear suddenly on the Earth delivered by an angel of God. The Bible was written by people just like us with some form of primitive inks and pens. They were divinely inspired in a way that none of us will fully understand in this life, but they were ordinary people with strengths and weaknesses. The Bible isn't a book; it is a collection of books. Seventy-three books in all - forty-six in the Old Testament and twenty-seven in the New Testament. Hence the name Biblia in Greek, which means the books or library. The Bible wasn't written all at once, nor was it all written by one person. In fact, 1500 years elapsed between the writing of The Book of Genesis and the writing of The Book of Revelation.

If you had lived at the time just after the death of Moses, you would have read from only five books, which we call the Pentateuch (the first five books – Genesis, Exodus, Leviticus, Numbers, and Deuteronomy). This was the embryo of the Bible.

It is perhaps needless to say that the Bible was not originally written in English, though the way some people represent it you might sometimes wonder. The prominent original language of the Old Testament was Hebrew and of the New Testament, Greek. What we have today is a translation into English from the original languages of the prophets, apostles, and evangelists.

In every case, it is important for us to realize that the cultures, countries, and times were very different than what we experience today. Some things can mean one thing in one culture and something quite different in another culture. I learned this very quickly as I began to travel from country to country in the earliest years of my ministry. In our own lives, we experience this in misunderstandings between generations as close as parents and children.

It is also critically important that we remember that the Bible, as we have it now, was not printed in any language at all until almost 1500 years after the birth of Jesus Christ. It is easy to forget in our modern world, where we can print and publish works from home computers, that not all ages have enjoyed the luxury and convenience of the printing press. For almost one and a half millennia after the life, death, and resurrection of Jesus, the only books that existed were hand-written. What type of perspective does that place on the modern Protestant-Evangelical idea that every person must carry around a Bible?

If you had lived prior to the invention of the printing press, like the men and women of the first fifteen hundred years of Christianity, you would have read the Scriptures from a manuscript that a Catholic monk or friar had laboriously copied onto pages of parchment or vellum.

Today, Protestants and Evangelicals are printing Bibles here, there, and everywhere, and shipping them off in every language to every continent in order to convert "the heathens." They do this in response to their self-imagined declaration that the Bible, and the Bible alone, can bring us salvation. So what happened to the people who lived before the Bible was printed? What happened to the people who lived before it was even written in its present form? How were men and women introduced to Jesus before the fifteenth century? How were the people of foreign lands inspired to live the Christian life before the Bible was available in mass-production? It is here, in the gap of most

Protestants' understanding of Christian history, that you find the beauty of Catholicism.

Does God have favorites? Did he favor those born after the fifteenth century more than those before? Surely God desired the countless millions of people who lived before the fifteenth century to know and follow the life and teachings of Jesus. But how could they if they had no Bibles, or had no money to buy Bibles, or could not read the Bible even if they could buy one, or could not understand the Bible even if they could read it?

From the Catholic perspective, salvation is available to the men and women of every age and every culture. Through the teaching of the Church, the people of every land for two thousand years have learned about the life and teachings of Jesus Christ. The people of every place and time have been encouraged to believe and do all that Jesus taught. And in many cases, this great work has been achieved in all corners of the globe without a written or printed Bible.

With this clear and concise understanding of the history of the Scriptures, the Protestant theory of "the Bible and the Bible alone" self-destructs into the most monumental case of well argued nonsense in the history of humanity.

Christians of all types around the world owe an enormous debt to the Catholic Church. The Catholic Church, inspired by the Holy Spirit, is responsible for the formulation, preservation, and integrity of the Sacred Scriptures. For fifteen hundred years, when there were no Baptists, Lutherans, Pentecostals, Methodists, Anglicans, Evangelicals, Non-Denominationals, or any other Christian Church of any type, the Catholic Church preserved the Scriptures from error, saved them from destruction and extinction, multiplied them in every language under the sun, and conveyed the truths they contained to people everywhere. Time and time again, heretics and apostates have tried to manipulate and corrupt these writings – and in some cases have done so, but the Catholic Church has preserved a version that is pure, complete, and free from the tamperings of man.

It seems strangely paradoxical that so many who claim to love Christ would be so hostile toward the Church, who has single-handedly protected the records of his life and teachings for so long.

The Bible is the most profound and sublime collection of writings in human history. It therefore goes without saying that these writings are also the most difficult to understand. Individual interpretation of the Bible is a very slippery path that leads people to great confusion, heartache, and distress. The history of Christianity in the last five hundred years is proof enough of this point. This type of approach doesn't promote unity, and always leads to division among Christians. What sadness Christ must feel as he stands witness to the bickering and division of Christian history. After all, in his final prayer he prayed "that all may be one" (John 17:22).

This is why the Catholic Church has, in her wisdom, so vigorously defended her sole right to interpret the meaning of the Scriptures throughout history. The living voice of the Catholic Church stands as a beacon for all men and women of good will, and announces the life and teachings of Jesus Christ with Tradition in one hand and the Scriptures in the other. Ultimately, interpreting the Scriptures comes down to a question of authority. It perhaps is no surprise that the greatest obstacle to Christian unity is also the question of authority. The greatest challenge that faces us, as Christians, in our quest for unity is to free so many from the blind subservience to a book and deliver them to a loving obedience to God alive and present in the one, holy, catholic, and apostolic Church.

Jesus

In every civilization, humanity has reached out to God. Deep in the heart of every person, there is a desire to know God and a yearning to draw nearer to him. Similarly, at every moment of human history, God has reached out to man. God desires to be with his people.

God's ultimate expression of this reaching out was the coming of Jesus Christ. Born two thousand years ago, Jesus of Nazareth is not a myth or a legend, but a well documented figure in history. But more than that, he claimed to be the Messiah who had been prophesied in the Jewish Scriptures – our Old Testament – and long awaited by the Jewish people. There is evidence to support this claim in his miracles, but ultimately we each must decide for ourselves – Was Jesus a liar, a madman, or the Messiah as he claimed to be? I suppose it is only by that mysterious and wonderful gift of faith that we are able to conclude that Jesus was who he claimed to be. I, am however, strengthened in my faith and forever intrigued by the fact that Jesus is the only person in history to have had his story foretold.

In books written as long as fifteen hundred years before Jesus' birth, people were already telling his story. Isaiah 11 prophesies that the Messiah will be born of the house of David. Matthew 1: fulfilled. Genesis 49 prophesies that the Messiah will be born of the tribe of Judah, one of the twelve tribes of Israel. Matthew 1: fulfilled. Micah 5 prophesies that the Messiah will be born in Bethlehem. Matthew 2: fulfilled. Isaiah 7 prophesies that the Messiah will be born of a virgin mother. Luke 1: fulfilled. Psalm 72 prophesies that kings will come to adore the Messiah. Matthew 2: fulfilled. Psalm 41 prophesies that the Messiah would be betrayed. Matthew 26: fulfilled. Zechariah 11 prophesies that the Messiah would be sold for thirty pieces of silver. Matthew 26: fulfilled.

Every noble human endeavor in history has been a preparation for the coming of Jesus or a response to the life and teachings of Jesus.

Jesus lived a life on this earth. He ate, he drank, and he walked down the street. Do you know him as a person? Or in your heart and mind, is he just a historical figure, a legend, or perhaps a myth? We must move beyond the façade of the story of Jesus Christ. We must delve deep into his life and teachings. We must allow his Spirit to flood the thoughts, words, and actions of our daily lives. In order to do all this we must come to know the Gospels intimately.

St. Jerome once wrote, "Ignorance of the Scriptures is ignorance of Christ." The great tragedy in the modern environment is that people know more about their favorite music group or sports players than they do about Jesus Christ. Get to know Jesus. Read the Gospels. Never let a day pass without pondering a few of the precious words in those four books. Don't just race through them. Read them slowly. Choose a small section and read it slowly. Then re-read it and ponder those words. Allow the words to penetrate the hardness of your heart. Allow the words of the Gospels to erode your personal prejudices, to wash away your narrow-mindedness, to banish your judgmental tendencies. You don't have to read five chapters a day, just a small passage. But allow the life and teachings of Jesus Christ, alive and present in the Gospels, to sink their roots deep into your life.

Imagine yourself there with dusty sandals, on those hot days, edging just to get a little closer, the crowds pressing in on every side. Only then will we form an intimate relationship with this man we call Jesus. Only then will we discover that he is God and Savior, but also coach, companion, mentor, guide, brother, teacher, healer, and friend.

The Power of the Word

You see, I believe the Word of God has the power to transform our lives. I have experienced this power in my own life and witnessed it in the lives of others. But I am convinced that the Word of God will not transform our lives through one quick reading on a Sunday morning in a church full of people where we are surrounded by a thousand distractions. In order to deliver its soothing waters to our souls, the Word of God needs to sink its roots deep into our hearts. This simply cannot take place under these conditions.

Let me ask you something, what was last Sunday's Gospel reading? Do you know? Do you have to think about it? Is it coming to you? Maybe you know and maybe you don't. My experience has been that ninety percent of Catholics can't tell you what last Sunday's Gospel was about.

If we don't know, I have to believe that it didn't and won't significantly impact our lives.

How does this happen? It is so easy to be distracted by any of a thousand different things at the moment when the priest begins to read the Gospel. All of a sudden, he is beginning his homily, and you have no idea what the Gospel was about. By the time Father has finished speaking, maybe you do and maybe you don't know what the Gospel was about... and chances are, you go home spiritually undernourished.

I will offer you one practical resolution that will dramatically improve your experience at church on Sunday and your relationship with God. The most powerful tool at your disposal to improve your experience of the Mass is preparation. We know the value of preparation in business, in school, and in sports, so why wouldn't the same be true when it comes to Mass? Preparation elevates every worthwhile human endeavor.

I would like to suggest that once a week, perhaps on a Tuesday or a Wednesday, you take time to read and reflect upon the coming Sunday's Gospel. If you are married, you may wish to share this experience with your spouse. Don't just rush through it. Read it slowly and pick out a word or a phrase that strikes you or jumps out at you. Take turns reading and take turns explaining which word jumps out at you. Then read it again. This time, be attentive for a word or phrase that strikes you. Maybe it will be the same word; maybe it will be a different word. It doesn't matter. Read the passage three times. If the Word of God is to transform our lives we need to allow it to sink its roots deep into our lives through repetition and reflection.

Each time, think a little about why that word is prodding you. Is there something happening in your life that this word or phrase speaks to? Is there something you should be doing that this word or phrase pricks your conscience? Perhaps something you shouldn't be doing and this word convicts you? That can be uncomfortable. Maybe a word comforts you? Inspires you? Whatever it is, let the Holy Spirit work in you.

Familiarize yourself with next Sunday's Gospel, and Mass will no longer be just part of your routine. It will become a spiritual experience and part of your adventure of salvation.

We love what we know.

When you get into the car, what songs do you want to hear on the radio? Songs you know. When you go to the theatre, what language do you want the play to be in? The language you know.

If you will apply this one resolution to your life, and practice this resolution with an open, honest, and humble heart, your whole experience of Mass on Sunday will improve tremendously. And little by little, you will begin to draw closer to the man whose footprints have left an indelible mark in the dusty paths of human history.

Stories

The greatest stories ever told are in the Bible, and every other story is only a variation of one of the Biblical tales that echo throughout history. They echo throughout history because they are the stories of men and women as they struggle to know themselves, to know God, and to work out their salvation.

Often people are shocked or surprised by the human weaknesses of the key characters in the stories of the Bible. Many are surprised, even scandalized that God would use people with such vices and shortcomings to reach out to humanity and give man hope in the future.

The danger is to read the Bible as an observer. It is easy to read these stories from the cold distance of an objective observer and not allow them to penetrate our lives. People have been doing just this ever since these stories were written. The challenge is to get involved.

It is all too easy to read the story of Moses leading the Israelites out of slavery and into the desert, and think that we have nothing to learn, or that we would never complain like the Israelites did when food was scarce. The temptation is to read the Gospels and believe that we would never be cruel, calculating, vindictive, and hard-hearted, like the Pharisees. We are tempted to think that we would be the one leper who returns. But the ultimate temptation is to read the Bible and see ourselves only in Jesus.

Every single person in the Bible is put there to serve you. This procession of people with their strengths and weaknesses, their faults, failings, flaws, defects, talents, and abilities, with their virtues and their vices, are your servants. Hidden between the lines of these ancient texts, they wait, wanting to teach you the great truths of the journey.

They provide the invaluable service of acting as mirrors. What do you see when you look into a mirror? Yes, yourself. These men and women afford you the opportunity to look deep into your divided heart and see your "self" – the good and the bad, that which is worthy and that which is in need of redemption.

Until you have learned to see yourself in every person in the Scriptures, you have not read the Bible.

The stories that fill the Bible are the stories of hundreds of men and women and their struggles to walk the path of salvation, to make the Journey of the Soul. They have tried to reach out and embrace the-best-version-of-themselves. In some of these characters, we find great success in this journey, in others we find great failure, but in most we find an intriguing mixture of both failure and success. Most draw near to God only to abandon his ways; then from the anguish of the brokenness and emptiness of their sin, they once again draw near to God and his ways.

There is perhaps no better example than Peter. One of the first to be gathered into Jesus' inner circle, Peter leaves everything behind to follow Jesus. Later, he turns his back on Jesus, denying he even knows him, but after Jesus' Resurrection, Peter becomes the unifying voice for the early Church.

Can you relate to Peter? Have you ever ignored what you knew in good conscience was the right thing to do because you were afraid what people might think of you?

As we discussed earlier, stories have a very powerful impact on our lives. Stories can transform civilizations. They can win wars or lose wars. Stories can conquer the hearts of millions. They can transform enemies into friends. Stories can help heal the sick. The proud despise them because they are simple, but stories are one of the most powerful agents in history. They can reform the political or spiritual temperament of an age. Stories can be either light or darkness. What stories are impacting your life?

Questions

The questions we ask in life are just as important as the answers we find. When we ask the wrong questions, we always find the wrong answers. Our modern culture is asking all the wrong questions, and that is why so many are living lives of quiet desperation. These are the questions we are encouraged to ask by this so-called advanced culture: What do I want to do? What's in it for me? Will it feel good? How can I get people to serve me? How can I do less and get more? How can I get more power? All of these lead us along the lonely path of self-centeredness. In this scenario, we place ourselves at the center of the universe. We place ourselves at the center of human history. Do we really expect to find happiness by building our lives on such a distorted view of life and reality?

As we read the Bible, we come across many people who fled from God's designs, but they never found happiness until they turned back to God and said, "Here I am Lord, I come to do your will" (1 Samuel 3:4). The greatest foolishness of man is the miscredited fantasy that we can find a lasting happiness separate from the will of God.

The questions we ask are important - questions we ask of ourselves, the questions we ask of our spouses, the questions we ask of our children, our employees and employers, our friends, and the occasional pilgrim stranger who crosses our path.

Questions are an important part of the spiritual journey. The temptation is to despise uncertainty. But uncertainty is a spiritual gift designed to help you to grow. From time to time, great questions arise in our hearts and our minds. Don't let your heart be troubled. Learn to enjoy uncertainty. Learn to love the questions. The questions are life.

Three or four years ago, my brother Andrew gave me a copy of a book entitled Letters to a Young Poet. It is a small book that contains a collection of letters written by the great German lyric poet Rainer Maria Rilke to Franz Kappus, who at the time was a young aspiring poet. In one of the letters, Rilke penned some words that have remained ingrained on my heart since I read and underlined them in that small volume. "Be patient toward all that is unresolved in your heart and try to love the questions themselves like locked rooms and like books that are written in a foreign tongue. Do not now seek the answers, which cannot be given you because you would not be able to live them. And the point is, to live everything. Live the questions now. Perhaps you will then gradually, without noticing it, live along some distant day into the answer."

Try to enjoy the wonder of the questions in your life. Allow your soul to breathe deeply, as the body must do sometimes to live amidst certain circumstances. Stand amidst the uncertainty of the great questions life proposes, take a deep breath, and enjoy them.

Finally, when you are reading the great stories of the Bible, if you happen upon God asking a question, take extra care. God has no need to ask questions, so when he does, he doesn't ask for his sake, he asks for ours. He asks questions like a great teacher. God asks questions to educate.

A great example of this divine questioning is in the third chapter of Genesis. God arrives in the garden at the time of the afternoon breeze as he did each day. Only on this particular day, Adam and Eve have hidden themselves. God calls out to them, "Where are you?" (Genesis 3:9). He doesn't ask because he doesn't know where they are. He asks because he wants them to realize where they are. God wants Adam and Eve to realize the absurdity of trying to hide from him. He wants them to be aware that they have turned their backs on him, gone against his life-giving designs, and rejected his friendship. By calling out to them, "Where are you?" he causes them to realize where they are and where they should be.

I often hear his call in the moments of the day. I find myself wandering from the path, and he calls to me, "Where are you?" I pray you too can learn to hear his gentle voice in the circumstances of your daily life.

Prayers

Woven into these ageless stories and the great questions the Bible raises in the human heart and mind, we also find some of the most beautiful prayers ever written. When you are confused or troubled, weary or distracted, and finding it difficult to concentrate during prayer, use these prayers. I often use a Psalm as my last prayer of the day. I kneel beside my bed and just pray the words of the Psalm slowly. Sometimes I go through them one after another, day by day. At other times, at the end of a long day I just turn to one of my favorites in search of guidance or comfort.

The Bible is the richest treasury of prayers. Some of the prayers are obvious, like the Psalms, but others are treasures hidden amongst the stories, waiting to be discovered. Amidst the hustle and bustle of my often busy days, I like to use what I call the "First Christian Prayers" to keep me in tune with my spiritual priorities. The First Christian Prayers is the name I have given to the words people spoke to Christ during his lifetime. When we pray, we speak to God and listen for God. These words were spoken directly to Jesus – true God and true man – so I believe they have a special power.

When I sense that God is calling me to something, but I'm not sure what, or when I have a decision to make and don't know which option to favor, I pray the words of the blind man, "Lord, open my eyes so that I may see" (Matthew 20:33). I pray them over and over in the moments of the day, using them as a mantra in the gaps between activities – at the stoplight, in line at the supermarket, when I am on hold on the telephone.

During times of doubt, questioning, or confusion, I use the prayer of the father of the possessed boy, "Lord I believe, help my unbelief" (Mark 9:24).

At other times I use the words of the criminal next to Jesus on the cross, "Jesus, remember me when you come into your Kingdom" (Luke 23:42).

And one of my very favorite prayers are the words of Peter when Jesus asks him three times, "Do you love me?" and Peter replies, "Lord, you know all things, you know that I love you" (John 21:17). Sometimes I use these words when I have offended God with my words or actions, or just simply been less than the person I was created to be. When my sinfulness overwhelms me, I pray, "If you wish you can make me clean" (Matthew 8:2).

I pray these simple prayers over and over again throughout the day. They allow me to keep connected to God even amidst the busy activity of each day.

———

The Bible is filled with many wonders. Embrace this rare treasure and allow its contents to draw you nearer to God and transform your life.

"Dad, if you really love me..."

Once upon a time, there was a young man. It was a little more than a week before his eighteenth birthday when he stopped by his father's office one afternoon. He hadn't been agreeing with his father on too many things lately, and he walked into his office and said, "Dad, it's gonna be my birthday next week, and if you love me you'll get me a new car for my birthday. And if you really love me, you'll get me the car I've always wanted." Then, without giving his father a chance to reply, he left.

The next morning, the boy's father said, "Michael, yesterday when you stopped by the office, you didn't mention what sort of car you've always wanted." Michael replied, "You know Dad, the red Porsche 911 turbo Carrera." The boy's father smiled and asked, "And, how much do they cost?" "Ninety-two thousand dollars, and if you really love me Dad, that's what you'll get me for my birthday. Don't let me down," Michael replied and left for school.

Tuesday came, and as was the family custom, they celebrated Michael's birthday with dinner and the cutting of the cake. And as they enjoyed their cake, one by one Michael's brothers and sisters each handed him a gift. He opened the gifts and thanked each of his family graciously, but his mind was elsewhere. Finally, the moment he had been waiting for arrived. Even as Michael's father handed him a rectangular parcel, he hoped he would find in it the keys to a brand new red Porsche.

Michael took one rip at the parcel's wrapping and discovered that it was a book – a Bible. Disgusted, he stood up, pushed his chair away from the table and against the wall, and rushed from the dining room. Racing upstairs to his bedroom, he slammed the door and threw the still unopened gift against the wall. It hit the wall, then the floor, and bounced into the corner.

Michael went to bed without talking to anyone, rose early the next morning, and took himself off to school.

Just before lunch that day, Michael's father suffered a massive heart attack. He was rushed to the hospital, and arrangements were made to bring Michael from school to the hospital to be with him. For seven hours, he sat at his unconscious father's bedside, playing the events of the night before over and over in his head. Then he got up and went to get some coffee and a sandwich, and while he was gone his father died.

Michael was devastated. He went home and lay on his bed and cried. He wept and wept for hours, and then out of the corner of his eye, he saw the gift still mostly wrapped over in the corner.

Getting up off the bed, he went to the corner and picked up the gift and finished unwrapping it. For some time he just sat there holding the leather Bible and staring at it. Then, opening the Bible, he discovered an inscription on the inside front cover.

Dear Michael,
Within these pages, you will find
the answers to all of life's questions,
and the secrets to all of life's sucesses.
With love on your eighteenth birthday,
Dad

He wept some more. The tears streamed down his face, falling to the page and smudged his father's handwriting. To console himself, Michael opened the Bible, searching further for some words to comfort him, only to discover that his father had placed a bookmark in the Bible. He removed the bookmark and stared at it with open-mouthed amazement. It was a check for ninety-two thousand dollars.

CHAPTER SIXTEEN

FASTING

As a human being, you are a delicate composition of body and soul. Your body and soul are carefully linked by your will and intellect. In its present form, your body is temporal. One day it will be buried, and it will decay. However, your soul is eternal. With all this in mind, it makes sense that you are going to be dead for a lot longer than you are going to be alive. And so, it follows that what is eternal should lead what is temporal. Yet it is so easy to allow yourself to be seduced by the things of this world.

The body and the soul are constantly vying for dominance. You wake up, and the body cries out, "feed me," so you eat. A couple of hours later the body cries out, "I'm thirsty," so you drink. Later the body cries out, "I'm tired," so you rest. Again the body cries out, "feed me," and you do. When it's time to exercise your body cries out, "I don't feel like it," so you don't. And at the end of the day, the body calls out, "I'm ready for bed," so you sleep. Whether we are aware of it or not, the body is ordering us around most of the day. The body is always crying out, feed me, sleep me, please me, pamper me, nourish me, wash me, relieve me, water me... In the modern climate, most people's bodies are winning the battle for dominance between body and soul.

In a sense, the body is like money – a great servant, but a horrible master.

The Death of Discipline

The present culture is allergic to discipline. The notion of freedom proclaimed by the modern world is anti-discipline. But true freedom cannot be separated from discipline.

The most obvious example of this paradox is in our cultural approach to dieting. For more than a decade now, the diet industry has been among the fastest growing industries in any sector of the economy. Every day, more and more products stock the shelves, and infomercials cram the airwaves.

All of these programs claim to perform wonders, and yet, if you've been to the beach lately, you can see that for the billions of dollars we spend on such products, we are still growing more and more overweight as a culture with each passing year. But now it has gone from the bizarre to the absurd!

If you think about it, what is it that people are looking for in these diets and diet products? And why do so many people fail in their approach to dieting?

As I have observed it, people want a diet that will allow them to eat whatever they want, whenever they want, yet still allow them to look great, feel great, and lose that undesired extra weight. Basically what they are looking for is a miracle product that will remove the need for any discipline in their eating habits, so that they can continue to indulge in their hedonistic ways.

Diets don't fail because the program wasn't any good. Diets don't fail because the product wasn't any good. Diets fail because we lack the discipline to adopt a program of eating and exercise that nurtures and promotes our maximum potential as a human being.

Moderation is the only diet most people need, but we seem to lack the inner strength to choose what is good, true, and right for us.

We want what is good for us, but we lack the strength of will to choose it. This problem is not new or unique to the modern world. Men and women of every age have experienced this same difficulty. And this is one of the reasons that for thousands of years, men and women have been practicing a variety of spiritual exercises to strengthen their will.

One such exercise is fasting.

Fasting in the Scriptures

For the Hebrew people, fasting was infrequent and was usually employed as a sign of repentance. The Torah requires only one day of fasting each year – Yom Kippur – which is the Day of Atonement. Four extra days of fasting were added to the Jewish tradition much later to commemorate the events leading to the destruction of Jerusalem.

The Israelites fasted at Samuel's urging, as they put away the false gods of Baal and Ashtaroth and returned to Yahweh (cf. 1 Samuel 7:2-6). The entire Israelite army employed fasting as part of its preparation for battle (cf. Judges 20:26 & Chronicles 20:3-4). Daniel fasted as he prayed, asking God to grant him the ability to understand the Scriptures (cf. Daniel 9:3). At the urging of Jonah and to save the city of Ninevah, the king proclaimed a fast, calling on the people to abandon wrongdoing and violence (cf. Jonah 3:7-9).

In each of these cases, fasting was used to humble oneself before God. Over and over again, the Old Testament makes it abundantly clear that genuine fasting involves turning away from evil and turning back to God. Fasting that involves no such conversion of the heart is useless. Isaiah speaks out against fasting detached from conversion, announcing the worthlessness of fasting in the wrong spirit (cf. Isaiah 58:3-7). The Scriptures continually remind us that external actions are insufficient. These external actions must be joined to some internal conversion of the heart.

―⁓⁓―

The New Testament also shines light on the ancient spiritual practice of fasting. On several occasions, the life and teachings of Jesus provide further insight into the meaning of authentic fasting.

Before Jesus began his public life, he was "led by the Spirit into the desert" where he fasted for forty days (Matthew 4:1). Jesus didn't fast in atonement for his sins; he was sinless. He fasted in preparation for his mission. And the fact that Jesus was "led by the Spirit" out into the desert to fast, is perhaps the greatest evidence we have that fasting is not merely a physical practice or just another personal accomplishment; rather, it is a spiritual exercise.

In the desert, Jesus is tempted by the devil to abandon his fasting and have his fill. Jesus rebukes him, saying, "One does not live on bread alone, but on every word that comes forth from the mouth of God" (Matthew 4:4). Fasting is a sharp reminder that there are more important things in life than food. Authentic Christian fasting helps to release us from our attachments to the things of this world. It is often these worldly attachments that prevent us from becoming the-best-version-of-ourselves. Fasting also serves as a reminder that everything in this world is passing, thus encouraging us to consider life beyond death.

—⁓—

Later during his public life, Jesus was challenged and questioned as to why his disciples didn't fast like the disciples of John the Baptist and the Pharisees. In his response, he reveals one of the prime purposes of fasting: "Can the wedding guests fast while the bridegroom is with them? As long as they have the bridegroom with them, they cannot fast. But the days will come when the bridegroom is taken away from them, and then they will fast on that day" (Mark 2:19-20).

One of the prime purposes of fasting is to help us become aware of God's presence in our lives and in the world around us. Since Jesus – God and man – was already in their presence, the disciples did not need to fast in the way we do while Jesus was with them.

—◦◦◦—

Jesus instructed his disciples only once specifically concerning fasting. During the Sermon on the Mount in Matthew's Gospel, Jesus speaks of fasting in the same way he spoke of almsgiving and prayer. "When you fast, do not look gloomy like the hypocrites. They neglect their appearance, so that they may appear to others to be fasting. Amen, I say to you, they have received their reward. But when you fast, anoint your head and wash your face, so that you may not appear to be fasting, except to your Father who is hidden. And your Father who sees what is hidden will reward you" (Matthew 6:16-18).

As with prayer and almsgiving, Jesus calls us to remember that fasting is a spiritual exercise, and as such is primarily an action of the inner life. We do not fast to impress other people. We fast to cultivate the inner life. Fasting should be an occasion of joy, not a cause of sadness. Authentic fasting draws us nearer to God and opens our hearts to receive his many gifts.

—◦◦◦—

There is one other occasion when Jesus mentions fasting. In my own life, this has been the most important passage relating to this great spiritual exercise. I believe this passage holds one of the greatest practical spiritual lessons, and yet, most modern Bibles have removed this passage or altered it.

In Mark's Gospel, we are told of a man who brings his possessed boy to Jesus for healing. The father of the boy explains that he brought the boy to Jesus' disciples, but they were unable to heal him even though they were able to heal many others with similar afflictions. When Jesus arrives at this scene, he rebukes the unclean spirit, ordering it to come out of the boy, and the child was cured. The disciples were confused as to why they were not able to cast out the demon. So, when the crowd had dispersed and they were alone with Jesus, "his disciples asked him in private, 'Why was it that we could not cast it out?' And he told them, 'This kind of spirit can only be cast out through prayer and fasting'" (Mark 9:28-29).

You perhaps believe that in our modern age, people do not suffer from possession by demons. Don't be so sure. The demons of our modern age are just subtler than the demons of Jesus' time. I assure you that many a drunken man takes on the qualities of a man possessed by a demon.

—*ϕϕϕ*—

In my own life, I have known the demon of habitual sin. When I first turned to God in my late teen years, I was possessed by such a demon. I tried with all my might to wrestle with this demon, but nothing worked. I prayed, begging God to free me from this sin, but he didn't. I employed all the power of my will, but that didn't work either. Then one day I noticed this passage in Mark's Gospel, and at that moment I felt the hand of God upon my shoulder. Encouraged by the example of a friend, several weeks later I began to fast each Friday, eating only bread and drinking only water. I offered this fasting to God, asking him to liberate me, and it was then that God cast the demon of habitual sin from my life. I believe with my whole being that some demons in our lives can only be cast out through "prayer and fasting" (Mark 9:29). If you are suffering under the slavery of ingrained habits, turn to God through prayer and fasting. If you are being tormented by the demons of habitual sin, turn to God through prayer and fasting.

You are a delicate composition of body and soul. Fasting is to the body what prayer is to the soul. Indeed, fasting is the prayer of the body.

The History of Christian Fasting

After the death, Resurrection, and Ascension of Jesus, fasting quickly became an integral part of early Christian practice. At that time, several Jewish groups were fasting on Tuesdays and Thursdays. To distinguish their own practice, the first Christians fasted on Wednesdays and Fridays.

In the Judeo-Christian world, a fast day generally implied abstaining from food until the evening meal, which would be served after sundown.

While some people argue that fasting was not introduced into the Christian way of life for centuries, there is considerable evidence that this is not the case. In fact, fasting was a part of the earliest Christians' way of life. A very early manuscript known as the Didache, which outlines Christian practice and belief, recommends that Christians "fast for those who persecute you."

Fasting was also common among these early Christian communities in preparation for the sacraments including the Eucharistic meal and Baptism. In the case of adult Baptism, both the baptizer and the one to be baptized would observe a fast in preparation.

In the fourth century, the Church began to regulate the practice of fasting, and since then, the practice has changed considerably at different junctures. In the Middle Ages, distinctions began to emerge regarding the amount and kind of food to be taken on a fast day. It was at this time that it became a rule to abstain from meat, eggs, and dairy products on fast days.

The number of fast days gradually increased over the years, as the eves of major feast days and the Ember Days were designated as fast days. And while the number of fast days was increasing, dispensations were being granted for a growing number of reasons. All this conspired to make the whole practice of fasting more and more complex. These growing complexities tended to transform the practice of fasting into more of a legal matter than a spiritual practice, and they tended to move the focus from inner transformation to outward display. The motive for fasting began to shift toward obligation and away from conversion and penance.

While there have been many changes in the practice of fasting over the centuries, the Church's understanding of it has remained consistent. The great thirteenth-century scholar, saint, and doctor of the Church,

Thomas Aquinas, wrote of these three values of fasting: for the repression of one's concupiscence, or strong desires, of the flesh; for the atonement for one's sins; and to better dispose oneself to higher things.

It was perhaps in the monasteries that the purpose and goal of fasting were preserved throughout the ages. Here in the monasteries, it remained clear that union with God was the primary goal and purpose of fasting. It is this point that has been grossly under-emphasized throughout the ages. This was largely due to the erroneous view that union with God was a reward reserved only for a few saints and mystics.

In the modern age, we have also seen many changes in the practice of fasting. Prior to 1917, Catholics were required to fast throughout Lent except on Sundays, taking only one meal per day. Catholics were also expected to abstain from meat, eggs, and dairy products on all prescribed fast days, as well as all Fridays and Saturdays of the year. By the early 1950s, fast days for Catholics in the United States consisted of one main meal and two small meatless meals.

In 1966, Pope Paul VI warned of the dangers of a legalistic approach to fasting and offered some new direction for the practice of fasting in the modern era in his Apostolic Constitution on Penance. He reminded Catholics that the outward expression of fasting should always be accompanied by the inner attitude of conversion. In this document, Paul VI not only stressed the value of fasting and other forms of penitence, but also reminded Catholics everywhere of the importance the early Christians placed on linking the external act of fasting with inner conversion, prayer, and works of charity. In doing so, Paul VI echoed Saint Augustine's idea: "Do you wish your prayer to fly toward God? Give it two wings: fasting and almsgiving." Having reasserted the value of fasting amongst prayer and charity as the "fundamental means of complying with the divine precepts of penitence," Paul VI then simplified the regulations for fasting and abstinence and handed authority over to local bishops' conferences to establish guidelines according to their culture.

Here in the Unites States, the National Conference of Catholic Bishops issued a pastoral statement later that same year announcing, "Catholics in the United States are obliged to abstain from the eating of meat on Ash Wednesday and on all Fridays during the season of Lent. They are also obliged to fast on Ash Wednesday and Good Friday." The pastoral statement encouraged the faithful to continue the traditional practice of Friday abstinence and also urged Catholics to perform works of charity in the spirit of penance, including visiting the sick and imprisoned, caring for the indigent, and giving alms to those in need. At the time, this was a radical shift, which eliminated many of the old rules and regulations regarding fasting, abstinence, and penance. As a result, many Catholics felt they were no longer obliged to follow any specific penitential practices. Only a few were able to see the wisdom of the changes and realize that they were being called to a deeper spirit of penitential conversion.

Despite the fact that many modern Catholics have abandoned penance and particularly fasting, at every level the Church continues to affirm the great value of these practices as means for authentic spiritual growth. Throughout this modern era, popes and bishops have invited Catholics to fast and abstain, to pray and perform charitable works as time-tested ways of turning our attention toward God and the needs of our brothers and sisters. But amidst the abundance and great wealth of advanced modern nations like the United States, it is all too easy to be seduced into the self-absorbed lifestyles promoted by today's popular culture.

Today, fasting is more popular in secular circles than it is amongst Catholics. Many health enthusiasts are turning to periodic fasting for cures for everything from insomnia and headaches to depression. Others are adopting this ancient spiritual practice to "cleanse" the body of impurities such as oxidants and the excess chemicals used to fertilize our foods. Fasting has even found a place in many diet programs as a tool to achieve dramatic weight loss and proper weight maintenance.

I pray we can rediscover the value of this ancient spiritual practice as modern Catholics. Not for God's sake, but for our own. I am utterly convinced that if we are to develop the inner freedom to resist the temptations that face us in the modern world, we must learn to assert the dominance of the spirit over the body, of the eternal over the temporal. If the spirit within each of us is to reign, then the body must first be tamed. Prayer won't achieve this, works of charity won't achieve this, and power of the will won't achieve it. This is a task for fasting, abstinence, and other acts of penance.

Lenten Fasting

There is great wisdom in the Christian practice of fasting. Though Christian fasting has been largely abandoned, the one penitential practice that seems to have survived the turmoil of this modern era is that of Lenten Penance. Although, I suspect it is hanging on by a very thin cultural thread, which will break unless we can make people aware of the great beauty and spiritual significance of these acts.

As I have said over and over again in my books and talks, our lives change when our habits change. The Lenten experience is a perfect example of the Church's intimate understanding of the nature of the human person. The forty days of Lent are an ideal period for renewal. Lent is the perfect span of time to form new life-giving habits and abandon old self-destructive habits. But most of us just give up candy and, when Easter arrives, we are no further advanced spiritually than we were at the beginning of Lent.

Fasting and You

There is a war taking place within you. It is the constant battle between your body and your soul. At every moment of the day, both are vying for dominance. If you wish to have a rich and abundant experience of life, you must allow your soul to soar. But in order to do that, you must first tame and train the body. You cannot win this war once a week, or once a year, or even once a day. From moment to moment, our desires must be harnessed.

Penance, fasting, abstinence, and mortification should be a part of our everyday lives. For example, if you have a craving for Coke, but you have lemonade instead. It is the smallest thing. Nobody notices. And yet, by this simple action you say "no" to the body and assert the dominance of the soul assisted by the will. The will is strengthened, and the soul is a little freer.

Or, your soup tastes a little dull. You could add salt and pepper, but you don't. It's a little thing. It's nothing. But if it's done for the right reasons, with the correct inner attitude, it is a spiritual exercise. You say "no" to the body. In doing so, you assert the dominance of the spirit. The will is strengthened, and the soul is a little freer.

Never leave a meal table without practicing some form of mortification. It is these tiny acts that harness the body as a worthy servant, and strengthen the will for the great moments of decision that are a part of each of our lives.

Beyond these moments of mortification, we should each seek encounters with fasting and abstinence if we are serious about the spiritual life. Not because the Pope says to or because our local bishops conference advises it, but because it will help us to turn away from sin and turn to God. Fasting helps us to turn our backs on the-lesser-version-of-ourselves and embrace the-best-version-of-ourselves.

Perhaps you can fast one day a week - two small meals, one full meal, and nothing to eat between meals. Perhaps you can fast one day a week on bread and water. Or maybe all you can manage at this time is to give up coffee for a day. Maybe you can't even give up coffee for the whole day, maybe just for two hours. Friday has always been a traditional day of fasting, and I would encourage you to employ this tradition in your own way. Only you can decide what is right for you in this area.

Try not to be prideful about it. Come humbly to God in prayer, and there in the Classroom of Silence, decide upon some regular practice of fasting and abstinence. Then, from time to time, review this practice. If you feel called to add to it, add to it.

—◦◦◦—

It is also important to recognize that not all forms of fasting and mortification involve food. You can fast from judging others, or criticizing, or cursing.

Two powerful forms of mortification that helped me to grow tremendously were the practice of silence and stillness. Sit in the silence for twenty minutes. It isn't easy. That is why so few people pray. After you have become comfortable in the silence, be still for twenty minutes. Completely still. It is difficult. Yet I am convinced that silence and stillness are two of the greatest spiritual tools.

Fasting is a simple yet powerful way to turn toward God. If there is a question in your life – fast and ask God to lead you. He will. If you have a persistent sin that you just cannot seem to shake – fast. Some demons can be cast out only by prayer and fasting together.

Fasting is radically counter-cultural, but so is true Christianity.

The Universe and You

Until this point, I have avoided discussing the idea of fasting as a form of penance to reverse the effect of sin. I have done this because there is such a negative stigma that goes with this idea in our modern world. All the same, I would be remiss not to discuss it and try to shed some positive light on this idea.

Even before kindergarten, we are taught the governing laws of the universe. One of these is the universal law of cause and effect. Every cause has an effect. Every action has a reaction.

In a sense, the universe has a perfect accounting system. This is the wonder and perfection of God's creation. It is these laws that keep everything in balance and harmony. As a result, no debt in the universe goes unpaid. All debts must be settled.

This is where the ideas of penance and fasting are linked.

We practice penance not because we want to punish ourselves or destroy ourselves, nor is it because the Church wants us to feel guilty or have a poor self-image; but rather, we practice penance as an expression of sorrow and to be restored. We want to be all we can be. We want to be all God created us to be. We want to become the-best-version-of-ourselves.

It goes without saying that if you sit on the couch everyday for ten years and eat potato chips and drink beer, the effects of those actions will be poor health. To erase the gained weight and return your physical capacities to optimum, you would have to work out and watch your diet. Neither of these are enjoyable at first, but they erase the effects of the poor past actions that led you to become less than the-best-version-of-yourself.

The same is true spiritually. Every time we sin, it has an impact on our souls. You can't see it, but it's there. When you sin, you not only damage your soul but you also increase your tendency toward sin and your appetite for sin in the future.

It is true that God forgives our sins when we confess them in Reconciliation, but the effects these sins have had on our being must be reversed with some form of penance. Fasting is one spiritual practice that can help restore the soul to its intended beauty, reduce our tendency toward those actions that are self-destructive and sinful, and reduce our appetite for sin in the future.

Always a Means, Never an End

Fasting is a means, but never an end. The purpose of fasting is to assist the soul in turning back to God. The benefits of fasting are innumerable, but all these benefits are secondary to the desire to embrace God more fully in our lives.

Whatever form of fasting you decide to employ in your life, you will have good days and bad days. You will have successes and failures. Stick to it. Don't give up. If you fail, try again.

I was back in Australia at the beginning of Lent last year. On Ash Wednesday evening, the phone rang as I was walking past it, so I answered it. "Is that you, Uncle Matt?" a little voice said. It was my niece, Zoe. "How are you Zoe?" I asked. "I'm good, Uncle Matt." "What did you do today?" I inquired. "Oh... It was a busy day. I went to school, then I went to volleyball practice, then I came home and did my homework, and then we went to church and I got ashes."

"What did Father talk about at church?" I asked. "He talked about giving things up for Lent. Guess what I'm giving up, Uncle Matt," she said. "I don't know, what are you giving up this year?" "I'm giving up Coca-Cola."

"But Zoe, you really like Coca-Cola." "I know, but Father talked about giving up something that will be really hard. So I'm giving up Coke."

Two days later on Friday evening, I was at a basketball game with my two nieces, Emma and Zoe. Emma is the elder and she was about fourteen at the time, and Zoe is the younger and at the time she was twelve. Emma was playing in the basketball game, and Zoe was sitting next to me with five or six of her giggling little friends from school.

About mid-way through the second half, I looked over and Zoe was guzzling down a large bottle of Coke. I didn't say anything. I just smiled to myself and turned back to the game. But about five minutes later, I felt a tug on my shirt and a tap on my shoulder. "Uncle Matt, Uncle Matt, I forgot." "You forgot what, Zoe?" I asked. "Oh... Uncle Matt I forgot I gave up Coke for Lent and I just drank a bottle of Coke." I didn't say anything. I just looked at her and smiled. She sighed and said, "Oh, well. It's all over now. I'll have to wait 'till next year."

—◦◦◦—

Our lives change when our habits change. Our habits change when we make resolutions, remind ourselves of those resolutions, hold ourselves accountable to those resolutions, and perform those resolutions.

Sometimes we fail, but there is no success that isn't checkered by failure. Don't give up. Press on. Little by little.

The spiritual journey is not made a mile at a time. More often than not, the advances in the spiritual journey are too small even to measure. But they all add up to a lifetime of joy-filled challenges and an eternity in union with everything that is good, true, beautiful, and noble.

Our bodies are vehicles that God has given our souls to experience life in the material realm. Until you get a grip on your body, you will never get a grip on any area of your life.

CHAPTER SEVENTEEN

SPIRITUAL READING

Books change our lives. Most people can identify a book that has marked a life-changing period in their lives. It was probably a book that said just the right thing at just the right time. They may have been just words on a page, but they came to life for you, and in you, and because of them you will never again be the same. It is true, books change our lives. What we read today walks and talks with us tomorrow.

Earlier in our discussion of prayer and contemplation, we spoke of the cause-and-effect relationship between thoughts and actions. Thought determines action, and one of the most powerful influences on thought is the material we choose to read.

Reading is to the mind what exercise is to the body and prayer is to the soul.

An Ancient Tradition

Spiritual reading is an ancient tradition. It has existed in the Church for as long as we have had books to read. In fact, spiritual reading was practiced long before the printing press was invented. In those days, this spiritual tradition was mostly confined to the monasteries where the monks had access to manuscripts of the Scriptures and other great spiritual writings.

The goal of spiritual reading is to ignite the soul with a desire to grow in virtue and thus become the-best-version-of-oneself. Like all other spiritual exercises and activities, spiritual reading seeks to encourage us to live a life of holiness.

What Should We Read?

Reading of the Scriptures, especially the New Testament and in particular the four Gospels, obviously holds first place. It has been my experience that all men and women of good will take delight in the Gospels as they become familiar with them. They are the best education of the life and teachings of Jesus Christ. Nothing ignites the soul to imitate the Divine Master more than an intimate familiarity with the story of his life, work, and teachings.

The Old Testament can also be very valuable as a source of spiritual reading, though in this case some books are harder to draw nourishment from than others. In books such as Psalms and Proverbs, our hearts are easily stirred to live a worthier life and to strive for virtue through our relations with God, neighbor, and self. On the other hand, many of the historical and prophetic books require some rather serious preparation if we are to understand the culture and context in which they were written and their intended message.

Beyond the Scriptures, there are also a great many spiritual writers who can be of assistance to us in our adventure of salvation. These masters and mentors of the spiritual life are always available for consultation. The masters of this art are able to set aside the issues of the day and their own personal agendas, and place at the center of their writing the great Spiritual North Star. In their writings, you will always hear a call to become a better person. As you read their words, you will constantly feel challenged to change, to grow, and to become the-best-version-of-yourself. They are also very worthy mentors, and if you allow them into your life, they will reveal your defects for you with great discretion and kindness. They point out your weaknesses not to belittle you, but so that you might grow and become all you can be. They do this by holding a spiritual mirror before us and calling us to self-examination. Then they encourage us to make generous resolutions. They echo the universal call to holiness that best characterizes the work of the Holy Spirit in the Church and in our souls.

It is within these bounds that the classical definition of spiritual reading has been confined until now. But for the sake of the modern Catholic who finds himself or herself in the midst of the information age, I would like to stretch those boundaries a little, while at the same time keeping our sight firmly fixed on the goal of this ancient practice.

I believe there is also a place within the context of spiritual reading for us to study certain issues. I believe most fallen-away Catholics are separated from the Church over one issue. For some, the issue is contraception, for others it is abortion, and many modern Catholics have turned their backs on the Church over the issue of divorce. I suspect that ninety percent of non-practicing Catholics are not joining us each Sunday because of a very limited number of issues. With that in mind, we have a duty to study and know those issues so we can build the necessary bridges of truth and knowledge to allow them to return to Church.

If you want to grow in faith, identify the teaching of the Catholic Church that you find most difficult to understand and read about it. Study that issue. Get yourself a Catechism and read what it says, but then look up the source texts, and get to the heart of the matter. Read contemporary books about the issue. Don't read books by bitter authors who seek to tear the Church down. Read books by men and women of prayer who seek by their writing to reveal the truth and depth of the Church's teachings. Study that issue, and the wisdom and beauty of Catholicism will be unveiled before your very eyes. The issues are so few; study them.

When, Where, & for How Long

When I first began to take the adventure of salvation seriously, I was very fortunate that my path crossed with the path of a very holy priest. He was a man of prayer, struggling to grow in virtue, and clearly focused on striving to live a holy life. His only concern in any of my conversations with him was my spiritual growth. He would say to me, over and over again, "God is calling you to a life of holiness." In the context of Reconciliation, he would remind me that God calls us all to holiness. In our conversations about my struggles with prayer, he reminded me that I was called to holiness. When I asked his advice on situations in my personal life, and later in my ministry, he always reminded me that our number one concern must be to honor God's call to holiness in our lives and the lives of the people who cross our paths.

I say all this because he also used to suggest books for me to read. In each of them, I found worthy guides, spiritual masters, and grace-filled mentors who reinforced this teaching that God calls us to be all we can be, to become the-best-version-of-ourselves. God invites us to holiness.

"Fifteen minutes a day," he would say. "It's amazing how powerfully fifteen minutes with the right book can stir your soul."

In the morning, in the evening, at lunchtime, whenever you can, find fifteen minutes to nourish yourself spiritually and intellectually with a good book. Try to do it everyday at the same time. Perhaps it is before you go to work. Maybe it is in bed late at night. Then again, perhaps it is while you are eating your lunch. Find a quiet corner at work or at home and read. If you're not sure what to read, send me an e-mail and I'll send you a list of suggestions.

You don't need two hours of reading everyday, just fifteen minutes. Do it everyday. Make it a part of your lifestyle. Remember, Catholicism is not a set of lifeless rules and regulations. Catholicism is a lifestyle. Start to build that lifestyle. Read for fifteen minutes everyday, and it will become a habit... our lives change when our habits change.

Adult Education

One of the challenges that is staring the Church in the face is the great need for adult education. Several generations have now managed to pass through the Catholic education system with little more than an elementary understanding of Catholicism, if that. This in turn is having a devastating effect on future generations, who are of course their children.

We could, of course, dream up all types of elaborate adult education programs, but my proposal is that we encourage Catholic adults to read good spiritual books. We cannot make up for lost ground overnight, but fifteen minutes a day is as good as any place to start.

My proposal will no doubt be overlooked by most, and frowned upon by others, because of its sheer simplicity. Nonetheless, let me assure you the simplest solution is usually the best, and hidden in our ancient traditions we will find the solutions to most of our modern problems.

Spiritual reading is a perfect example of an ancient solution to a modern problem. For a moment, just imagine if every Catholic in your parish read a good spiritual book for fifteen minutes a day. How would your parish change? If every Catholic spent fifteen minutes a day, every day, learning about his or her faith, how different would our Church be in a year? Five years? Ten years?

Rome wasn't built in a day. Most great things are achieved little by little.

Keeping the Star in Sight

Spiritual reading is a great tool to help us keep the great Spiritual North Star in sight. When we view everything in relation to our call to holiness, everything finds meaning. Even the smallest and most menial tasks take on new life, for we come to understand that every action is a character-building action, for better or for worse.

Direct all your thoughts and actions toward the great Spiritual North Star. What I mean is, find ways of spending time with your friends that help you all become the-best-version-of-yourselves. Similarly, find activities you can do as a family that draw the best out of each of you and challenge you to grow. In the same way, read books that make you want to become a better person – books that show you how to become the-best-version-of-yourself. Cast off the whimsical modern reading materials. What is in those magazines that will help you live a richer, fuller life? When was the last time you read a newspaper and said to yourself, "I'm a better person for having read that newspaper!"? We have bought into the modern myth that we have to be up on everyone else's business.

Books change our lives. If you really want your life to change, read some good spiritual books. If you will approach these books with a spirit of faith, a desire to grow in holiness, and a sincere intention to practice what you read, spiritual reading will become a powerful spiritual tool in your life.

CHAPTER EIGHTEEN

THE ROSARY

Jim Castle was tired when he boarded his flight one night in Cincinnati, Ohio. The 45-year-old management consultant had put on a weeklong series of business meetings and seminars, and now he sank gratefully into his seat, ready for the flight home to Kansas City, Kansas.

As more passengers entered, the place hummed with conversation, mixed with the sound of bags being stowed. Then, suddenly, people fell silent. The quiet moved slowly up the aisle like an invisible wake behind a boat. Jim craned his head to see what was happening, and his mouth dropped open.

Walking up the aisle were two nuns clad in simple white habits with blue borders. He immediately recognized the familiar face of one of the nuns: the wrinkled skin, the eyes warmly intent. This was the face he'd seen in newscasts and on the cover of TIME. The two nuns halted, and Jim realized that his seat companion was going to be Mother Teresa.

As the last few passengers settled in, Mother Teresa and her companion pulled out rosaries. Each decade of the beads was a different color, Jim noticed. The decades represented various areas of the world, Mother Teresa told him later, adding, "I pray for the poor and dying on each continent."

The airplane taxied to the runway, and the two women began to pray, their voices in a low murmur. Though Jim considered himself not a very religious Catholic who went to church mostly out of habit, inexplicably he found himself joining in. By the time they whispered the final prayer, the plane had reached cruising altitude.

Mother Teresa turned toward him. For the first time in his life, Jim understood what people meant when they spoke of a person possessing an "aura." As she gazed at him, a sense of peace filled him; he could see it no more than he could see the wind, but he felt it, just as surely as he felt a warm summer breeze. "Young man," she inquired, "do you pray the rosary often?" "No, not really," he admitted.

She took his hand, while her eyes probed his. Then she smiled. "Well you will now." And she dropped her rosary into his palm.

An hour later, Jim entered the Kansas City Airport, where he was met by his wife, Ruth. "What in the world?" Ruth asked when she noticed the rosary in his hand. They kissed, and

Jim described the encounter. Driving home, he said, "I feel as if I met a true sister of God."

Nine months later, Jim and Ruth visited Connie, a friend of theirs for several years. Connie confessed that she'd been told she had ovarian cancer. "The doctor says it's a tough case," said Connie, "but I'm going to fight it. I won't give up."

Jim clasped her hand. Then, after reaching into his pocket, he gently twined Mother Teresa's rosary around her fingers. He told her the story and said, "Keep it with you, Connie. It may help." Although Connie wasn't Catholic, her hand closed willingly around the small plastic beads. "Thank you," she whispered. "I hope I can return it."

More than a year passed before Jim saw Connie again. This time, face glowing, she hurried toward him and handed him the rosary. "I carried it all year," she said. "I've had surgery and have been on chemotherapy, too. Last month, the doctors did a second-look surgery, and the tumor's gone. Completely!" Her eyes met Jim's. "I knew it was time to give the rosary back."

In the fall of 1987, Ruth's sister Liz fell into a deep depression after her divorce. She asked Jim if she could borrow the rosary, and when he sent it, she hung it over her bedpost in a small velvet bag.

"At night I held on to it, just physically held on. I was so lonely and afraid," she said, "yet when I gripped that rosary, I felt as if I held a loving hand." Gradually, Liz pulled her life together, and she mailed the rosary back. "Someone else may need it," she said in her note.

Then one night in 1988, a stranger telephoned Ruth. She'd heard about the rosary from a neighbor and asked if she could borrow it to take to the hospital where her mother lay in a coma. The family hoped the rosary might help their mother die peacefully.

A few days later, the woman returned the beads. "The nurses told me a coma patient can still hear," she said, "so I explained to my mother that I had Mother Teresa's rosary and that when I gave it to her she could let go; it would be all right. Then I put the rosary in her hand. Right away, we saw her face relax! The lines smoothed out until she looked so peaceful, so young." The woman's voice caught. "A few minutes later, she was gone." Fervently, she gripped Ruth's hands. "Thank you."

Is there special power in those humble beads? Or is the power of the human spirit simply renewed in each person who borrows the rosary? Jim only knows that requests continue to come, often unexpectedly. He always responds, though whenever he lends the rosary, he says, "When you're through needing it, send it back. Someone else may need it."

Jim's own life has changed, too, since his unexpected meeting on the airplane. When he realized Mother Teresa carries everything she owns in a small bag, he made an effort to simplify his own life. Jim says, "I try to remember what really counts – not money, or titles, or possessions, but the way we love others."

Why Have We Abandoned the Rosary?

There are perhaps many reasons why modern Catholics have abandoned the rosary. One reason is, no doubt, the overemphasis some people have placed on the role of Mary and the rosary. But I doubt very much that this is the whole reason that Catholics en masse have stopped praying the rosary and stopped teaching their children to pray the rosary in their homes and schools. And as I pointed out in our discussion of the saints, the solution to the distortion or overemphasis of a good is never to abolish the good in question.

I suspect one of the reasons the rosary has become so unpopular during this modern era is because it is stereotypically considered the prayer of an overly pious old woman with little education and too much time on her hands. In a world where we bow to knowledge and academic degrees, piety is considered to be bordering on superstition. Piety is reverence for God and devotion to God. Isn't part of the goal of every Christian life to devote oneself to God?

Catholics have abandoned the rosary today because we have been seduced by complexity. We give our allegiance and respect to complexity, but simplicity is the key to perfection. Peace in our hearts is born from simplicity in our lives. All the great leaders throughout history have agreed that usually the simplest solution is the best solution. The genius of God is simplicity. If you wish to tap into the wonder and glory of God, apply simplicity to your life and to your prayer.

Our lives are suffering under the intolerable weight of ever increasing complexities. We complicate everything. And as this diseased fascination with complexity has swept across modern culture, it has also affected the way we approach prayer. Subsequently, as modern Catholics, we have deemed the rosary worthless.

Don't despise simplicity. Simplicity is the key to perfection. There is real power in simplicity.

The rosary is not a prayer just for grey-headed old ladies with too much time on their hands. It is a rich practice of prayer that we can all benefit from.

Perhaps your objection is that you were forced to pray the rosary as a child. If this is the case, move beyond that experience and discover this beautiful prayer for yourself, fresh and anew. Don't let your past rob you of your future.

Benefits

Contrary to popular opinion, the first book I ever published was entitled *Prayer & the Rosary*. Now the fact that someone publishes a book about the rosary at the age of nineteen probably leads most people to assume that I grew up in one of those homes where the rosary was prayed together every night. I didn't. In fact, I have never prayed the rosary with my family. Not even once.

So, how did I come to have such a high regard for this simple prayer, which has been so ardently rejected by our sophisticated modern world?

Let me tell you.

When I was in fourth grade, Mrs. Rutter taught us how to pray the rosary and gave us each a pair of rosary beads. I didn't pay much attention and I wasn't much interested, but for some reason I kept the beads in a place with my childhood treasures.

In fifth grade, Mr. Greck spoke a lot about Lourdes, where his son had been miraculously cured, and every Friday he would lead the rosary in the chapel at lunchtime. If you got detention, you had to go to the rosary. I got detention occasionally, but the compulsory rosary didn't do much for my love of this prayerful devotion.

At sixteen, I met a man who was to become very instrumental in my spiritual journey. He was teaching a study-skills course that I was attending after school, and invited me one Saturday to visit a local nursing home. We walked to the nursing home and spoke about a lot of things, mostly about me, my sports, my part-time job, how much money I had saved, and my girl-friend. The experience at the nursing home that after-noon was the first of many encounters at the nursing homes in my area that would begin to form my moral senses. As we walked home that day, he asked me if I would like to pray the rosary. I agreed. I mean, what else can you do in a situation like that? But for some reason, the prayers soothed me, and I began to pray the rosary on my own in the days and weeks ahead. Not long after that, I began to pray the rosary regularly with my good friend Luke.

I began praying the rosary because it is a form of prayer that I find very soothing, both mentally and spiritually. Today, I pray the rosary because I believe it is the simplest way to reflect upon the life and teach-ings of Jesus Christ. To place this in the context of the Journey of the Soul, I believe that as Christians we are called to imitate Jesus. It is impossible to imitate some-one you do not know, but by praying the rosary in a rel-atively brief period of time, we can ponder many aspects of Jesus and his life. And the actions of our lives are determined by our last most domi-nant thought. If our actions are to be like those of Christ, then we must be pondering his life and teachings regularly.

We spoke earlier about the power of stories. There is no more powerful story than the story of Jesus Christ. This is the story that has formed and focused human history, and it is essential to our mission as Christians that we are intimately familiar with his story. The rosary helps know his story and integrate his story into our own lives.

Growth in Virtue

One of the primary and practical benefits of the rosary is its ability to help us grow in virtue.

As I have studied the great spiritual masters of our Catholic tradition, I have discovered how essential virtue is to the Journey of the Soul. When we connect the good and noble external acts of our lives with positive internal attitudes and intentions, we grow in virtue. As we begin to practice a virtue intentionally, it develops into a habitual virtue. But I have also learned that when you intentionally focus your energies toward growing in a particular virtue, you automatically grow in every other virtue. Virtue begets virtue. Eventually, the habitual effort to practice a virtue blossoms into spontaneous right action. I have found the rosary particularly helpful in my attempts to increase the practice of various virtues in my life.

The fruits of all spiritual exercises are an increase in the supernatural virtues: faith, hope, and love. St. Paul speaks of them in his first letter to the Corinthians, "So faith, hope, and love remain, these three; but the greatest of these is love" (1 Corinthians 13:13). At a time when the world is so filled with doubt and skepticism, the beauty of faith shines forth. With so many people's hearts and minds suffering with depression, despair, and hopelessness, the splendor of hope is radiant. In a culture that exults the selfish attainment of pleasure and possessions, one eternal truth remains clear to all - for everyone knows that love is the only way.

Beyond the supernatural virtues, with each decade the rosary introduces practical examples of human virtues, and teaches us to practice these virtues in our own lives.

Fifteen Lessons

The actions of your life are determined by your last most dominant thought. So turn your mind to those things that are good, true, beautiful, and noble – and your life will be a reflection of these things.

A calm mind is the fruit of wisdom. Calmness of mind is the result of the patient practice of self-control. I know few practices that will help you acquire this calmness of mind, heart, and spirit like the rosary will. And by learning to direct your thoughts toward God, you will learn to direct your life toward God.

In the rosary, we have fifteen mysteries that beget fifteen lessons in life, love, and the attainment of virtue.

—◦◦◦—

In the First Joyful Mystery – The Annunciation - we learn about the power of saying "yes" to God's will in our lives, as we witness Mary surrendering with her whole heart to God's designs for her life (cf. Luke 1:28-38).

In the Second Joyful Mystery – The Visitation - we learn the value of service as Mary leaves her home to attend to her cousin Elizabeth (cf. Luke 1:39-42).

In the Third Joyful Mystery – The Birth of Jesus - we encounter the humility of Jesus, the Son of God, born in a stable (cf. Luke 2: 1-7).

In the Fourth Joyful Mystery – The Presentation - we witness a powerful example of obedience, as Mary submits her child, the Son of God, to the Law of Moses (cf. 2:23-32).

In the Fifth Joyful Mystery – The Finding of Jesus in the Temple - we learn that true wisdom does not come from the mere attainment of knowledge; but rather, is a gift from God (cf. 2: 45-49).

–––

In the First Sorrowful Mystery – The Agony in the Garden – we learn the importance of perseverance in prayer (cf. Luke 22:41-45).

In the Second Sorrowful Mystery – The Scourging at the Pillar – our spirits are renewed for the sacrifices of each day, and we learn never to despise the little things and the value of attention to detail (cf. John 19:1).

In the Third Sorrowful Mystery – The Crowning with Thorns – we learn compassion for those who are mocked and rejected, and we ask forgiveness for the times we have added to the insults of others (cf. Matthew 27: 27-30).

In the Fourth Sorrowful Mystery – The Carrying of the Cross – we are moved to help Jesus carry his cross by standing up to injustice and influencing our environment in a positive way (cf. John 19:17-18).

In the Fifth Sorrowful Mystery – The Crucifixion – we experience the pain evil causes and feel the weight of our own sins (cf. Luke 23: 42-46).

—⁓—

In the First Glorious Mystery – The Resurrection – we are reminded of the reality of life after death, and we learn to live with that in mind (cf. Mark 16: 1-7).

In the Second Glorious Mystery – The Ascension – we are reminded of the great commission to continue the work of Jesus on Earth (cf. Mark 16: 15-20).

In the Third Glorious Mystery – The Descent of the Holy Spirit – we are reminded that we are assisted in our efforts to do good by the unfathomable power of the Holy Spirit alive within us (cf. Acts 2: 1-4).

In the Fourth Glorious Mystery – The Assumption - we are reminded of the beauty of purity (cf. Revelation 12:1 & 17).

In the Fifth Glorious Mystery – The Crowning of Our Lady Queen of Heaven – we learn to honor and seek the counsel of those who attain virtue in their lives (cf. Song of Songs 4:7-12).

More than One Way

There is more to praying the rosary than just saying the rosary. Anyone can say the rosary. Just teach them the words, and they can rattle them off. But to genuinely pray the rosary, we must have a clear objective in our minds. The rosary is not magic. There is no deal-making to be done with God. So many rosaries don't equal a prayer answered by God.

Prayer doesn't change God; prayer changes us. We should approach prayer seeking to understand God more, rather than seeing prayer as an opportunity to give God his instructions for the day. We should approach prayer with the hope of growing in virtue.

There are many different practical approaches to the rosary. The first, of course, is to focus on the words. The words of the rosary are deeply rooted in the Scriptures and Christian tradition. The Our Father was of course given to us by Jesus himself (cf. Matthew 6:9-13). The Creed represents the first expression of Christian conviction. The first part of the Hail Mary comes from the message delivered by the angel to Mary in Nazareth: "Hail, full of grace. The Lord is with thee" (Luke 1:28). This greeting is then followed by the words Elizabeth used to greet Mary during the Visitation: "Blessed art thou among women, and blessed is the fruit of thy womb" (Luke 1:42). The Glory Be is the simplest expression of Christian belief in the triune God. And from the times of antiquity, Christians have placed themselves under the name of God and the sign of redemption, thus giving us The Sign of the Cross.

The words of the rosary are powerful and filled with meaning, but so are the mysteries that we use as a backdrop to each decade.

One thing is certain, your mind cannot do two things at once. This is where many people become discouraged with praying the rosary. They try to pray the words and meditate on the mystery at the same time.

Impossible! We must decide between the two, choosing one or the other.

On those occasions when you choose to meditate on the mysteries, allow the words to float by. Get lost in the scene. Imagine yourself there.

When you choose to focus on the words, it may help to meditate on the mystery for three or four minutes before each decade.

I also find it very fruitful to unite an intention with each decade. Offering each decade for a person or a situation helps me to stay focused, and avails me the opportunity to pray for many people in my life.

There are some people who think that we should pray the rosary everyday. In my own life, there have been months, even years, when I have prayed the rosary everyday. At other times, weeks and months have passed without praying the rosary. Generally, I have discovered that when I make time for this simple but profound practice of prayer, I am a better person. I seem to have certain calmness and awareness, which make me more readily disposed to living a life of virtue.

I don't think we need to enter the debate of whether or not every Catholic should pray the rosary everyday. I do, however, think that all Catholics should be able to bring forth the rosary from their spiritual storehouse from time to time as the Spirit prompts them.

Our prayer lives should be dynamic, like love. Our love should be constant, but express itself in many different ways. So it is with prayer. Learn to allow the Spirit to guide you to the type of prayer that will most benefit you on a particular day. Not the type of prayer you "feel" like doing, but the type of prayer that will

most benefit you on that day, depending on the disposition of your spirit.

Mary

Mary is the most famous woman in history. She leads
all prominent women who have earned their fame by a
life of virtue. She has inspired more art and music than
any woman in history, and even in the modern age, she
fascinates the imaginations of men and women of all
faiths. In our own age, Mary has appeared on the cover
of TIME magazine more often than any other person.

I suspect that, if we are to reconcile the great dishar-
mony that exists between the role of men and the role
of women in modern society, we will need the insight
of this great feminine role model. Is it possible for us to
understand the dignity, value, mystery, and wonder of
women, without first understanding this woman?

But beyond her fame and her historical importance
is her centrality to Christian life. The first Christians
gathered around her for comfort and guidance, yet
modern Catholics treat her like she has some contagious disease. One of the great challenges that we face
as modern Catholics is to find a genuine place for Mary
in our spirituality.

PART FOUR

NOW IS OUR TIME

The challenge that presents itself to the Catholics of every age is to transform every environment. It is all too easy for us to say that our time is more difficult than some other time. All periods of history have unique situations and challenges. Ours is no different. The people of every age think that their time and place is special, and that their circumstances are extraordinary. They are not. Humanity faces the same challenges in every age. They may come wearing different masks, but they are essentially the same.

There is great wisdom and genius in Catholicism. The human heart yearns for happiness, and God wants us to be happy. But we only experience this happiness, and the fulfillment that accompanies it, when we are changing, growing, and becoming the-best-version-of-ourselves. Catholicism is the dynamic program and lifestyle that assists us in this transformation.

The benefits of this transformation are not confined to the individual. When Catholicism is lived as it is intended to be, it elevates every human activity, every human person, and every human environment that it touches.

In 1517, when Martin Luther started the Reformation, there was no doubt that the Catholic Church was in need of reform. But reform should have come from within. Today the Church is in need of reform again. I pray that this reform will be the result of the flourishing caused when you and I embrace the ancient tradition we call Catholicism in a dynamic way, and thus, become the-best-version-of-ourselves.

CHAPTER NINETEEN

TIME FOR A CHANGE

For almost ten years now, I have been traveling the world and speaking to men, women, and children of all ages and cultures. During this time, I have been blessed with the opportunity to see more of the world than most presidents, and more of the Church than most bishops. I suspect these rare experiences have produced in me a unique perspective, but I hope that the ideas that make up this perspective resonate also in your heart.

I love the Church. To me, Catholicism is a gift that cannot be described. It must be experienced to be fully appreciated. My travels have affirmed one thing above all else, and that is, people love the Church. The press may attack the Church, fallen-away Catholics may ridicule the Church, and even practicing Catholics may criticize the Church, but I firmly believe these are just distorted expressions of love and admiration. Sometimes love goes sour, as it has for many modern Catholics. When love goes sour, it is usually for one of two reasons: misunderstanding or selfishness.

It is true that the Church has many problems at this moment in history. These problems fill my heart with a great sadness, but they do not lead me to despair. I see them as opportunities for us to change and grow. I see them as a chance for us to envision once again what it truly means to be Catholic.

Are We Willing to Change?

The circumstances of this moment in history have conspired to present this proposition to the Church: Change or more of the same?

Nature teaches us that everything in this world is constantly changing. Change is one of the laws of the natural universe. Everything God created is constantly in the process of either growing or dying. History also teaches us that those who try to prevent change and avoid change always fail.

While these laws of change are true of the natural realm, we also experience supernatural realities. Faith, hope, and love are perfect and personal examples.

Amidst this dynamic and ever changing natural environment, we also experience truth. And truth is unchanging. The environment changes, the culture changes, people change, but truth does not change, and God does not change.

The question therefore, is not, Will the Church change? For it certainly will, just as it has in every century for two thousand years. The question is not, Should the Church change? The problems and dilemmas we face are proof enough of that. The question is, How should the Church change in the twenty-first century?

To answer this question, it is important to understand that the Church is the connection between two worlds. The first world is the supernatural world. The second is the natural world, as we know it. In one hand, the Church holds truth - eternal and unchanging. In the other hand, she holds the practices that encourage and enable us to apply unchanging truth to the ever changing circumstances of our daily lives.

So before we get overly-excited about the changes that we think the Church needs to make, or the changes that we think need to be made to the Church, it is important that we understand what constitutes authentic change. Most of all, we need to develop an intimate understanding of the relationship between any particular issue and the eternal and unchanging truth that guides the Church's position on that issue.

What the Church most certainly does not need, is change for the sake of change. And we do not need change that is driven by philosophies such as Individualism, Hedonism, Minimalism, Relativism, and Materialism. We are where we are today because we have allowed these self-centered philosophies of compromise to direct change in the Church over the past thirty years.

Some believe the answer is to go back to the model of Church in the 1950s. Others would like to drag us all the way back to the Middle Ages. I promise you, the answer is never to go back. Throughout salvation history, God himself teaches us this lesson. Adam and Eve were blessed to experience Eden, but were banished from the garden for their own good after they disobeyed the guidelines God had given them for their own good (cf. Genesis 3:23). In the fullness of time, God sent his only Son to redeem humanity (cf. Galatians 4:4 & John 19:30). After this reconciliation, God didn't send us all back to the Garden of Eden. No, he imagined something new and greater. God never goes back, he always moves forward.

The story of salvation never goes backwards, it is always marching forward. The answer is never to go back, the answer is always to move forward.

How should the Church change in the twenty-first century? We must learn to bring forth both from the old and the new (cf. Matthew 13:51). A simple reorganization is not going to do it. We need some radical change, but not in the way that most people might think. When "change" and "the Catholic Church" find themselves together in a conversation these days, more often than not people are talking about the reintroduction of married priests, allowing divorced Catholics to once again receive the sacraments, reviewing the Church's position on contraception, and changing the nature of the role women play in the Church. All of these issues are peripheral to the real challenges that face us.

It is true, we need change. But we need authentic change that will bring forth genuine fruit, season after season. We need to start educating Catholics about their yearning for happiness and the role discipline plays in the fulfillment of that yearning. We need to show people in practical ways how we are happiest when we allow the timeless insights of the Gospel to direct our actions. We need to rediscover the abundant riches of Catholic spirituality. We need to provide answers to the pressing questions of our age and the common objections to Catholicism, answers that people can understand. We need to intelligently articulate the relevance of Catholicism in the modern world. We need to encourage lay Catholics to actively participate in the mission of the Church. And above all, we need to become prayerful people, and thus, a people of prayer. In a word, we need to inspire people. We need to inspire people to live life to the fullest (cf. John 10:10). We need to inspire people to follow Christ.

Change is necessary and inevitable. Rather than allowing "the spirit of the world" to direct us, I pray we allow the life-giving "spirit of God" to direct this change in the Church and our own lives.

—◦◦◦—

If you don't think something needs to change, go to Church next Sunday and look around. Then ask yourself, "Where are the young people?" Not the very young, but the twenty-somethings and thirty-somethings. At twenty-nine years old, I find myself right in the middle of what is now statistically the largest age-segment of Catholics in America, and yet, the least practicing segment of Catholics in America.

For the most part, they went to Catholic schools and were raised in Catholic families. But somewhere along the way, something went drastically wrong. Somehow we have failed to communicate the value of living a life of virtue and faith. In some way, we have failed to communicate that walking with God is the best way to live. We have failed to demonstrate the relevance of Jesus and the Church in the modern climate. And unless we can do this, and do it convincingly, they will not be back anytime soon.

―――

Are we willing to change? I hope so. Every person I speak to says, "The Church really needs to change." What we perhaps forget in making this statement is that we are the Church. And so, the real question becomes, Are you willing to change? Are you willing to become the change the Church needs? It has been my experience that most people are not. We appoint ourselves experts, criticize from afar, and use the Church's shortcomings as excuses not to get involved.

You know how hard it is to change yourself. Just take one tiny aspect of your own life as an example. Pick a bad habit you have and try to replace it with a good habit. How long does it take? How many times do you fail before you finally succeed? So be patient with the Church, which is two thousand years old and made up of 1.2 billion people. Change will come slowly, because the Church will change for the better only as quickly as you and I grow in virtue and become the-best-version-of-ourselves.

What Should We Focus On?

If the Catholic Church is to change and grow and thrive in this modern climate, it will be for one reason: because we become a more spiritual people. Only then will this renewed spiritual health burst forth into authentic action.

Authentic Catholic education and genuine evangelization will cause the whole Church to blossom, for it is impossible to know God and not love him. Those who do not love God simply do not know God. And it is equally impossible to experience God and not want others to experience him as a result.

It seems clear that the active part of our work as Catholics in the twenty-first century should be focused on two areas: education and evangelization.

Education

Sooner or later, someone is going to start suing Catholic high schools and colleges for false advertising. How is it possible that so many can pass through the Catholic education system and know so little about the Church, Catholicism, and indeed, Christ?

The Catholic education system as a structure is one of the marvels of modern society. It is the cause of envy amongst countless other groups and organizations and anyone with an agenda to push dreams of getting access to the Catholic education system. Why? Because they realize how powerful it could be if it was actually employed. That's why it is under attack, and that's why so many people have forced their agendas upon the Catholic education system. All the while, we have failed to use it for the good it was created to produce in students, families, and society.

Do we want to teach our children about Jesus, the value of virtue and character, and the beauty of the Church? Or do we just want privileged educational environments to teach them what they need to get into the best colleges? Do we want to prepare them for life? Or do we just want to prepare them to become cogs in the global economic wheel? Do we believe that by teaching them about Jesus and the role the Church can play in their lives that we are better preparing them for college and for life? Or have we resigned ourselves to "the spirit of the world?"

Catholic education is one of the great wonders of modern civilization. It is unprecedented and it is genius. That is why it has been imitated by every other religious organization on the planet. They know the power of the Catholic education system. But the Catholic education system is misemployed and under-employed in these modern times.

—⟿—

Education in any context is best directed by questions. Many educators throughout the ages have tried to impose their views on others. Such teachers, if they can be called that, tend to lecture. That is to say, their style is a monologue. But true teachers are not trying to impose their views on the student; but rather, they are trying to draw out the truth. Great teachers propose questions. That is to say, their style more resembles a dialogue.

The questions we ask are as important, perhaps more important, than the answers we find. If we ask the wrong questions, we will always find the wrong answers. If Catholic education is to change in a way that is authentic and life-giving, it will do so only because we choose the right questions to base Catholic education upon.

In modern society, the position of the Church is now habitually questioned and doubted. The teachings of the Church are ridiculed by self-appointed "experts" who know little or nothing about the Church and the wisdom that forms her teachings. This cultural mood is the number one enemy of Catholic education.

If you want to win a war, there are three things you need to know. Firstly, you need to know you are at war. Secondly, you need to know who or what your enemy is. And finally, you need to know what weapons and strategies can defeat your enemy.

Our enemy is ignorance. It is amazing how many degrees you can award in a culture and still have the masses completely ignorant of the truth. Ignorance of the truth is the enemy of the Church, Catholic education, and indeed Christ.

If we will take the time to study the teachings of the Church, we will discover in them a rare beauty and a profound wisdom. Some may argue that the teachings of the Church are too difficult to understand. Truth was never designed for the twenty-second sound bite. We have that against us in a sound-bite driven culture. But in the context of a Catholic school, we are not confined by twenty-second time limitations. Instead, we have years to explore the wonders of the essential questions regarding life and faith.

Instead of questioning the Church's teachings with no effort to understand her point of view, or simply dismissing the Church's view as outdated and old-fashioned, perhaps we should try to understand her position.

Do we actually believe that we know better than the collective towering genius of Catholic philosophers and theologians of the past two thousand years? How did we become so proud and arrogant that we question these extraordinary men and women without hesitation or investigation? What is our basis for our position? Is it simply that we find the teachings of the Church inconvenient?

If we had keen minds and keen spirits, if we were truth-seekers, we would genuinely ask, "Why does the Church teach what she teaches about...?"

This is the question that should shape Catholic education. Perhaps we should allow high-school students to raise all the questions about Catholicism and all the objections they have heard against the Church. Then, in each case, let us ask this question together, "Why does the Church teach what she teaches about that?"

We should not ask this question with the sarcastic, cynical, and even dismissive tone that many ask it with today in academic circles. They ask it as if the question itself were an answer. We should ask this question with the greatest confidence. We should ask it knowing that before too long, the fruits of thousands of years of great practical, intellectual, and spiritual wisdom will eclipse before our eyes, hearts, minds, and souls. This kind of spiritual and intellectual eclipse is a life-forming experience, a life-changing moment, and a life-directing influence. If we could expose each Catholic high-school student to just one such experience, they would have a newfound respect for the great wisdom of the Church. If we could show them the truth, and the beauty of that truth, in relation to just one of their questions or objections, we would infinitely elevate their love and understanding of the Church. They may still wander away from the Church, they may still act contrary to the teachings of the Church, but deep in their hearts they will know that the Church is not merely another earthly human institution, but rather, a divinely appointed custodian of truth and wisdom.

Let's face it, there are probably only a dozen issues that are being used by this modern secular culture to rob today's Catholics of their faith. Would it be that hard to put together a textbook that clearly answers the objections, articulately outlines the Church's position, and explains the modern relevance of each of these issues?

We may not be able to explain everything about Catholicism, but we shouldn't let what we can't do interfere with what we can do. If we can develop a love of truth in young Catholics and empower them to seek truth, we will have served them rightly. To do this, we must stimulate within them a positive form of curiosity. The ultimate curiosity. Curiosity for truth. This quality so akin to the philosopher will guide them morally and ethically through life. Truth-seekers always end up with God. It is much harder for those who are indifferent to truth, or deny the existence of objective and unchanging truth, to come to know God.

There is great beauty in the truth. If only we could harness the energies of the Catholic education system to show young people how this truth can set them free (cf. John 8:32). Only then will we be able to show them the beauty within themselves and have them believe us. Authentic love of self and genuine self-esteem are born from right relationship with God and the truth he has revealed.

Educators, parents, politicians, and psychologists all seem to agree that one of the largest, and quite possibly the largest, problem amongst young people today is poor self-esteem. You cannot correct this problem by simply showering a child with compliments. Self-esteem is born from right relationship with God, others, and self. This relationship with God and everyone and everything in the universe, is developed by an ever increasing awareness of the truth. It is truth that sets us free.

I hope we can learn to value truth again, even amidst this culture of appearance and deception.

The truth is beautiful. When we read it, when we experience it, our souls soar. As John Paul II put it so poetically and powerfully in his 1993 Encyclical Letter, Veritatis Splendor, "THE SPLENDOR OF THE TRUTH shines forth in the works of the Creator, and in a special way, in man, created in the image and likeness of God (cf. Genesis 1:26). Truth enlightens man's intelligence and shapes his freedom, leading him to know and love God."

The Catholic education system is perfectly positioned to ignite within the hearts and minds of young Catholics a sense of passion, awe, and hunger for truth. It is critical that we reassess at this juncture what we wish to bestow upon those who attend Catholic schools. If it is simply an elite education for a privileged few, then surely we are in direct conflict with the Gospel that we claim to be guided by. But if we wish to bestow upon our children the values and beliefs that emerge from the life and teachings of Jesus Christ, then clearly it is time for a change.

The ironic thing is that most young people are looking for someone who has the courage to look them in the eye and tell them the truth. Young people want above all to be their own person. But they want to be the-best-version-of-themselves. And they need and want guidance in their lives.

The Catholic education system has the potential to play an unfathomable role in the renewal of the Church. More than any other activity in the Church, it has a rare opportunity to reorient modern men and women toward God. In order to actualize its potential, the Catholic education system must simply do what it claims to – offer a Catholic education.

Evangelization

My experience has been that most Catholics today are uncomfortable with the word evangelization. The reason is because the term "evangelization" has been kidnapped by Protestant-Evangelical churches, and their methods of evangelization are often quite argumentative, intimidating, and forceful. Apart from these, a number of self-promoting and self-serving television "evangelists" seem to have been linked with every imaginable scandal over the past twenty years. Not only have they kidnapped the term evangelization, but they have also kidnapped the term Christian. Amazingly, many modern Christian churches don't even consider Catholics to be Christian. That's like saying Coca-Cola isn't cola. Nonetheless, the issue before us is evangelization, which is in essence to share the Gospel with other people.

Organizations have a tendency of becoming preoccupied with the day-to-day pressures, problems, and programs. The danger in this is that we lose track of what we are trying to accomplish. It is for this reason that most institutions, from colleges to multinational businesses, are constantly reviewing and revisiting mission statements, core values, long-term goals, short-term goals, and overall strategic plans.

If you went into an ice-cream store and there was no ice-cream, you'd say, "There's a problem!" If you went to a chocolate store and there was no chocolate, you'd say, "There's a problem!" The mission of the Church is to share the Gospel, and to teach, challenge, and encourage people to become more like Jesus Christ. So how is it that we can belong to a local church community that goes on year after year with almost no outreach to the unchurched in the area, and with very few people really becoming more Christ-like, and yet think there is no problem? Let me tell you, if this describes your church community, "There's a problem!"

I suppose what it really comes down to is whether or not we sincerely believe that knowing and following

Christ is the best way to live. I suspect that, on some level, most Catholics don't. Because if we did, we would most likely be more excited to share it.

The nature and purpose of the Church is to influence people and communities in a positive way. A local church community should be contagious. Everyone who belongs to that community should be reaching out both actively, with efforts to evangelize, and passively, with the example of their lives.

—◦◦◦—

One thing seems more than apparent, and that is, we need a strategy. Today's Catholics are not just going to drift into a more Christ-centered lifestyle on their own. Our church communities are not going to become contagious overnight. We need a strategy, because these types of things only ever happen on purpose!

Allow me to suggest a simple four-step plan.

STEP ONE. In the first place, we must begin to nurture friendships. Friendship was the original model of evangelization. The first Christians did not seek to spread the faith by means of political power, and they didn't have the use of the mass-media. They simply engaged the oldest and most reliable method of influence – friendship.

Every year, advertisers spend millions of dollars to create a positive perception for their products. But every advertising executive up and down Madison Avenue knows that the word-of-mouth endorsement of a friend, someone you know and trust, will influence your decision more than any advertisement ever will.

We live in a culture in which spiritual authorities and religious institutions are increasingly questioned, distrusted, and ignored. But fortunately, friends still listen to and trust friends. Visit any culture on any continent, and you will discover this universal human dynamic: friends listen to friends.

STEP TWO. The second step in our evangelization strategy is to pray for the people we are trying to reach with the life-giving values, principles, and ideas of the Gospel.

Prayer is powerful. Prayer is essential. Prayer cuts through and clarifies. Prayer gives us vision, courage, strength, and endurance. Prayer dissolves our prejudices, banishes our narrow mindedness, and melts away our judgmental tendencies. Prayer erodes our impure motives. Prayer opens people's hearts to God and his ways.

Our work to share the Gospel with others should never be separated from our prayer for those people. For if this separation occurs, we run the great risk of falling into the pursuit of personal agendas.

STEP THREE. The third step in our strategy of evangelization is to tell your story.

Stories change people's lives. The stories of Francis of Assisi, Mother Teresa, John Vianney, Thomas More, and John Paul II have had tremendous influence on my life. Their stories have changed my life, but the stories of hundreds of ordinary people that I have met along the way have also greatly impacted me.

We have already discussed the great power of stories in Chapter Eleven. Now you need to discover your story. We all have a story - the sequence of events that led us through doubts and questions to a time and place where we came to believe that right-living is the only way to be happy. That doesn't mean we don't still sometimes have doubts and questions. Nor does it mean that we are not attracted to things and actions that are self-destructive from time to time.

Tell your story. Despite how ordinary you may think it is, you will be amazed how easily people will relate to your journey, and be inspired by it. Despite all your faults and failings, there is real power in your story.

STEP FOUR. Finally, the fourth component of this evangelization strategy is to invite your friends and neighbors to outreach events at your church.

This proposes a problem in most Catholic communities. The problem: we don't have outreach events. Some may argue that we have the RCIA program for those interested in exploring Catholicism. But this program runs for months. What we need are some monthly or quarterly programs that parishioners can invite their family, friends, and neighbors to attend. Programs that inspire. Programs that ignite a little passion in people for right-living. We need outreach programs, and they need to be relevant and innovative.

One of the major barriers to Catholic evangelization is the lack of outreach events. Protestants and Evangelicals can just invite their friends to church on Sunday. But Catholics won't. Why? Because it becomes really awkward around Communion time when everyone is going to receive and you have to tell your friend that he can't. Result: he doesn't feel welcome, he feels left out, and he never comes back.

When was the last time you showed up to a party you were not invited to? People are not comfortable coming to events where they don't feel welcome. And the truth is, there are a lot of Catholics who don't feel welcome in the Catholic Church. As Catholics, we need to engage the power of the invitation. We need to invite people.

And once they are there, we need to make people feel welcome. Whether we were the ones who invited them or not, we need to go out of our way to help people feel welcome in our Church, to make them feel like they belong. This sense of belonging is important to all of us. If people don't find this sense of belonging in their local Catholic church, they will go to another church where they do feel like they belong.

—◦◦◦—

Perhaps this strategy is too simple, but I am convinced that we need a step-by-step strategy that is specifically geared toward reaching the people in the modern culture we are living and working in.

The early Church was unstoppable, and for all I can tell, it was because they followed this simple strategy. They believed that the values and principles of the Gospel were the best way to live. They nurtured friendships. They were deeply committed to a life of prayer. They were courageous in telling their story. They invited people to outreach events – although they probably didn't call them that - and they made people feel welcome in their communities.

The people of today desire happiness just as the people the first Christians were reaching out to did. So, we come back to the question, Do you believe that knowing and following Jesus is the best way to live? Because you and I are not spectators in the great mission of the Church. We are participants. Let's be practical for a moment. How can you help others to discover the beauty and value of the life and teachings of Jesus Christ?

We can fulfill our call to share the Gospel by teaching our children and by living the values and principles of the Gospel in our own life. But we also have a unique opportunity to share the life-giving teachings of Christianity with our friends. No one is better positioned to touch your friends with the beauty of truth and faith than you are. We learn more from our friends than we ever will from books. Each of us influences the lives of our friends more than we could ever imagine. Whether we are aware of it or not, we are all exerting a tremendous influence upon the people that we spend time with. Let me ask you, are your friends better people because they know you? Are you helping your friends become the-best-version-of-themselves? Are you living your life in such a way that those who know you, but don't know God, will come to know God because they know you?

The great vehicle that God wants to use to share the truth, beauty, and wisdom of his ways with the modern world is not the mass-media or the Internet. The vehicle God wants to use is friendship.

Friendship is the original model of evangelization, and friendship is the model of evangelization that will triumph in the modern context. It is only through friendship that trust and mutual respect are established, which together bring about the openness and acceptance that give birth to vulnerable dialogue. Only then can we begin addressing the questions that every human heart longs to answer. Who am I? Where did I come from? What am I here for? How do I do it? Where am I going?

Friendship is the key to evangelization.

How can you practically apply these ideas to your life?

Sometime today take a few moments in the Classroom of Silence, and ask God to point out five people in your life who could benefit from a greater knowledge and appreciation of God and the Church.

Write down the names of those five people. Mentally attach one of their names to each finger on your right hand.

Pray for those people everyday for the next month. Pray for each of them by name. Everyday. Make yourself available to God. Tell him that you would like to help them discover the benefits of living a life of virtue.

After the month of prayer is finished, call each of them up and make arrangements to spend an hour or two with each of them individually. Take them to lunch, go for a walk, play golf, or meet for coffee. When you have this time with them, one to one, talk to them about what is going on in the different areas of their lives.

Do this once a month with each of the five people. For three months, don't talk about God, religion, or the Church unless they introduce the topic to the conversation.

After the three months have passed, during one of your monthly visits, invite them to join you on a visit to a local homeless shelter, soup kitchen, or nursing home. Go to these places and help out, or just visit with the people there. Nothing awakens the moral, ethical, and spiritual senses like encounters with the underprivileged.

Then, and only then, having formed the friendship and developed some level of mutual respect, begin the dialogue about the place God has in our lives. This mutual respect is essential to the process of evangelization. Without it, you will speak but people will not listen. But with this mutual respect established, even if they disagree with you, they will listen to you and weigh your point. At least then, the truth will have a chance to settle on the good soil in their hearts (cf. Mark 4:8).

Over time and as the dialogue continues, give them a good book about the spiritual life - a book that will challenge them to think, to change, to grow, and to become the-best-version-of-themselves. Then in your future get-togethers, talk to them about the ideas in the book.

When the time is right, invite them to join you for an outreach program at your church. Afterwards, invite them back to your place for brunch or coffee and talk about the program.

Continue to foster these friendships, and God will use you powerfully. I will never forget the people who did just this for me. Without their time and effort, without their passion for the life-giving ways of Christ, I don't know where I would be today. I am eternally grateful to them. And one day your friends will be eternally grateful to you.

—⁓—

It is impossible to be living a Christ-centered life and not want to share the wisdom of right-living with others. I pray we will embrace virtue more and more in our own lives. And I pray we will begin to share the infinite treasures of the Church with others more enthusiastically.

The great evangelization that is needed will not take place via the mass-media. It will take place through the simple and timeless treasure of friendship. This is the original model of evangelization, and it is still the most effective.

Vocations

Life is vocational. We all have a vocation. And it is in finding and following that vocation that our restless hearts find rest. Our vocation is God's intimate response to your individual desire for happiness. He places within you the desire for happiness, and he calls you to that happiness you desire with a specific vocation. Such is the genius of God.

In many modern nations, we are experiencing a great shortage of priests at this time. The crisis is much greater than most are aware. The situation is so dire that statistics suggest that if something does not change, fifteen years from now half the parishes in America will not have a resident priest.

What is the solution to this problem? Some say we should reintroduce a married clergy. There is certainly precedence for this all the way back to the first disciples. Others say we should ordain women. There is no precedence for this in our two-thousand-year history, so I think it is unlikely. Jesus showed he was more than willing to cross all types of social boundaries, so I suspect it is so for a reason.

Why is there such a great shortage of priests? I believe the primary reason is because we have stopped preaching the Gospel. Maybe one out of ten times do I come out of church on a Sunday and think to myself, that homily really challenged me, inspired me, convicted me, and showed me the changes I need to make...

We have stopped preaching the Gospel. We are preaching for the lukewarm. Paralyzed by fear, we have watered down the message so much that most Catholics struggle to find the relevance. It is true in our schools, it is true in our colleges, and it is true in our churches on Sundays. I may be accused of being critical, but unless we are willing to admit we are failing, we will never succeed. Until we are willing to admit we have big problems, we will not turn our efforts to finding big solutions.

Young people want to give their lives to something worthy. They may not be consciously aware of this desire, but nonetheless, they are moved by this desire. Young people don't want to be shown the path of compromise and least resistance. They want to be challenged to be all they can be. They want to be guided in the paths of truth, virtue, and happiness. They want to be coached to become the-best-version-of-themselves. In short, they want to know the Gospel.

If we preach the Gospel, we will have vocations. If we live the Gospel, our seminaries will begin to overflow. Nothing is surer.

CHAPTER TWENTY

LEADERSHIP

People need leadership, and in the absence of genuine leadership, they will listen to anyone who steps up to the microphone. People want leadership, but when they perceive that leaders are self-serving, they reject them and assume the role themselves. They realize they are not qualified, but they would rather go to their peril under their own leadership than under the leadership of an unauthentic leader.

As Catholics, we are desperate for some authentic leadership. Fifty years ago, people gave their allegiance and support to people in positions of leadership merely because they had a position of prominence or authority. Not anymore. People don't respect authority today. In fact, they question it, they are skeptical of it, and they are cynical toward it.

Does it not strike you as a great poverty of leadership that, here in America, we cannot put one person on the evening news who can be acknowledged by Americans from coast to coast as a Catholic leader? It is true that the late Cardinal O'Connor was very effective in harnessing the media in New York and establishing a vibrant identity as a Catholic leader on the East coast. It is also true that Cardinal Mahony has done the same on the West coast, and that the late Cardinal Bernadin was able to do so in the mid-west. Many lay Catholics who occupy positions of prominence in the business world, the entertainment world, or the political realm, have successfully established a Catholic identity in different regions. But we have no national figures. Not within the clergy and not amongst the laity. Does that not strike you as a massive poverty of leadership?

All this has become self-evident in the midst of the recent controversies that have enveloped the Church. Why are we unable to put forth even a single national Catholic figure who can speak to the issues of the day clearly and articulately, in a way that is bold, brilliant, and inspiring?

Perhaps we are doing it the wrong way. It is possible that our whole system of organization that has helped us in the past is now hurting us. Perhaps the provincial model of administration and organization – parish, diocese, and archdiocese, under Rome – is hurting us in a time when the whole world is quickly becoming a global village. On top of all this, when talented leaders do emerge, we don't help and empower them; we make their paths almost impossible.

Why are we so unwilling to raise these leaders up when they do emerge? Why do we keep them down? Why do we regionalize them? Why do we persecute them? Are we afraid they will become too popular? Are we afraid we won't be able to control them? Whatever the reason, we should try to pinpoint it, because in the absence of this desperately needed leadership, the Church will have to content herself with mere survival. We must address the issue of leadership. If the Catholic Church is to thrive in the twenty-first century, it will because of bold and brilliant leadership guiding people toward the great Spiritual North Star.

The fact that we cannot put forth a single spokesperson who can be nationally recognized to speak about different Catholic issues in a bold, brilliant, articulate, and inspiring fashion should send up a red flag.

Something is amiss.

Paralyzed by Fear

There is a great fear that has seized the leadership of the Catholic Church. I am not referring only to bishops and priests, but also to lay leadership. Fear has paralyzed our leadership.

The rapid change in the world over the last seventy-five years caught the Church almost completely unprepared. Six hundred years passed between the invention of the plow and the invention of the automobile. Only sixty years passed between the invention of the automobile and the space age. It is during this period of rapid change that the whole model of Church was challenged by a culture that completely re-oriented the hearts and minds of humanity.

Before this rapid period of change, many men were humbled by their lack of education and accepted the authority, teachings, and leadership of the Church based upon faith. But by the mid-1960s, the devastating impact of enlightenment thinking was beginning to have its effect on everyday men and women. From that time on, men, women, and children of modern western nations have been taught to question absolutely everything.

It is this "questioning" that caught the Church unprepared and that put the Church on the back foot. This defensive posture was the beginnings of the fear that has seized the Church. The Church was simply unable to adapt to these changes fast enough. We were unable to retool and refocus our educational institutions fast enough to respond to the new demands of the modern intellect. We were unable to reeducate our clergy and religious in such a way that they could respond to the changing criteria of the modern mind. As a result, we find ourselves continuously on the back foot, perpetually in the defensive position, struggling just to survive.

Stifled by this fear, over the past fifty years too many of our leaders have hidden behind inaction, using discretion, prudence, and discernment as their excuses. There is a difference between fear and discretion. There is a difference between fear and prudence. There is a difference between fear and discernment. Fear is not a virtue.

The most common phrase that appears in the New Testament is, "Do not be afraid." The most common phrase that appears in the Old Testament is "Be not afraid," Together, in the Old and New Testaments, this phrase appears more than 1,000 times. Do you think God is trying to get a message across to us?

Courage

The most dominant emotion in our modern society is fear. We are afraid. Afraid of losing the things we have worked hard to buy, afraid of rejection and failure, afraid of certain parts of town, afraid of certain types of people, afraid of criticism, afraid of suffering and heartache, afraid of change, afraid to tell people how we really feel... We are afraid of so many things. We are even afraid to be ourselves. Some of these fears we are consciously aware of, while others exist subconsciously. But these fears can play a very large role in directing the actions and activities of our lives. Fear has a tendency to imprison us. Fear stops more people from doing something with their lives than lack of ability, contacts, resources, or any other single variable. Fear paralyzes the human spirit.

Courage is not the absence of fear, but the acquired ability to move beyond fear. Each day we must pass through the jungles of doubt and cross the valley of fear. For it is only then that we can live in the high places – on the peaks of courage.

Take a moment to wander through the pages of history – your family's history, your nation's history, human history – and extract from those pages the men and women whom you most admire. Who would they be without courage? Nothing worthwhile in history is achieved without courage. Courage is the father of every great moment and movement in history.

I have felt the chilling winds of fear and self-doubt rush against my skin. I have discovered that courage is learning to recognize and master that single moment. That moment is a prelude. A prelude to courage or a prelude to fear. So much can be accomplished in one moment of courage. And so much can be lost to one moment of fear.

No one is born with courage. It is an acquired virtue. You learn to ride a bicycle by riding a bicycle. You learn to dance by dancing. You learn to play football by playing football. Courage is acquired by practicing courage. And like most qualities of character, when practiced, our courage becomes stronger and more readily accessible with every passing day. Virtues are like muscles, when you exercise them they become stronger.

Everything in life requires courage. Whether it is playing football, or coaching football; crossing the room to ask a girl out on a date, or rekindling a love that has grown cold; starting a new business, battling a potentially fatal disease, getting married, struggling to overcome an addiction, or coming humbly before your God in prayer - life takes courage.

Courage is essential to the human experience. Courage animates us, brings us to life, and makes everything else possible. And yet, courage is the rarest quality in a human person.

The measure of your life will be the measure of your courage.

Bold Leadership

What we need is bold leadership. Goethe, the famous German writer, once wrote, "Be bold and mighty forces will come to your aid." It is this boldness that the Church needs. And I promise you that whenever and wherever a leader emerges with this boldness, the people will clamor to support such leadership. They will respond like people dying of thirst who have just been offered a cool drink of water. It will be as true for a local pastor in his parish as it has been for John Paul II on an international scale. The people are desperate for authentic leadership. They are lost and lonely like sheep without a shepherd.

People don't follow titles and authority. They follow courage.

There is boldness in Catholicism when it is truly lived. People are hungry for the truth, but we are afraid to give it to them. The truth will set them free, but we don't have the courage to proclaim it (cf. John 8:32).

In the last chapter, I shared, "The ironic thing is that most young people are looking for someone who has the courage to look them in the eye and tell them the truth. Young people want above all to be their own person. But they want to be the-best-version-of-themselves. And they need and want guidance in their lives." This is true not only of young people, but of all people.

Where will this courage we so desperately need come from? Perhaps the answer lies in the lives of our spiritual ancestors – the saints. They were not timid, whimpering, and non-committal. They were brave and bold. Why? They knew their essential purpose. They moved always in the direction of the great Spiritual North Star. They formed habits that helped them become the-best-version-of-themselves. They knew that happiness was impossible separated from the ways of God. And they took the opportunity to share the truth and wisdom of Catholicism with others seriously. Where did they get all this from? Prayer. In its many forms, prayer nourished their lives.

Cervantes' counsel was this: "He who loses wealth loses much; he who loses a friend loses more; but he who loses courage loses all." Shakespeare wrote, "Virtue is bold, and goodness never fearful."

To be a Catholic leader is a position of spiritual leadership, and therefore, the primary concern of a Catholic leader must be dedication to the spiritual life. I've never met a prayerful coward. Virtue is bold, goodness is not fearful, and prayerful leaders are courageous leaders. And courage, like every other virtue, is contagious.

Servant Leadership

Some people think of Jesus as just a good guy, others as a prophet, some as a sage, and others yet, as God and Savior. At one level or another, Jesus is universally admired. Yet, few people consider him as a relevant leadership model for their lives.

Jesus gave birth to a method of leadership that had never been seen before. Throughout history, all the great kings, queens, and emperors have measured their strength, power, and greatness by their wealth and the number of servants they ruled. But Jesus, the greatest leader of all time, did not come to be served. Jesus came to serve.

"He rose from supper and took off his outer garments. Then he took a towel and tied it around his waist. Then he poured water into a basin and began to wash the disciples' feet and dry them with the towel around his waist.... When he had washed their feet and put his garments back on and reclined at table again, he said to them, 'Do you realize what I have done for you? You call me "teacher" and "master" and rightly so, for indeed I am. If I, therefore, have washed your feet, you ought to wash one another's feet. I have given you a model to follow, so that as I have done for you, you should also do'" (John 13: 4-15).

Even some of his disciples were expecting him to use his power to rule in some earthly capacity, but again Jesus' methods of leadership were very different than anything that had ever been experienced before. For thousands of years, kings, queens, and emperors had been sending their people off to die for them. Jesus was the only leader who decided to die for his people.

Jesus' whole method of leadership focused on turning the hierarchy upside-down. The model of leadership that Christ himself left us was one of service and sacrifice.

—◦◦◦—

If you use your power to make people do things they don't want to do, you are not a leader; you are just a dictator or a tyrant. If you can inspire people to do things that are difficult, but good for them and their community, then you are a leader.

The most effective leaders are authentic leaders. In Chapter One, we discussed how in our own time there is an abundance of leaders standing at the crossroads pointing us down a path they have never traveled themselves. But what we need is authentic leaders. Men and women willing to lead humanity along the right path with the example of their own lives. Authentic leaders lead by example.

The laws of authentic leadership seem to have been universally proven throughout human history whether in business, in battle, in the sporting arena, or in church. I think we find a reasonable summary in the following anonymous quotation:

"I submit to you that leaders will never be more or less than their soldiers' evaluation of them. This is the true efficiency report. From most of your troops you can expect courage to match your courage, guts to match your guts, endurance to match your endurance, motivation to match your motivation, esprit to match your esprit, a desire for achievement to match your achievement. You can expect a love of God, a love of country, and a love of duty to match your own. They won't mind the heat if you sweat with them, and they won't mind the cold if you shiver with them.

You see, you don't accept the troops; they were there first. They accept you. And when they do, you'll know. They won't beat drums, wave flags, or carry you off the drill field on their shoulders, but you'll know. You see, your orders will appoint you to command. No orders, no letters, no insignia of rank can appoint you as a leader. Leadership is an intangible thing. Leadership is developed within yourselves; and you'll get stronger as you go."

—⁓—

At different times, we are called upon as leaders. Some as mothers and fathers, others as CEOs and presidents, and others yet, as priests and bishops. Whatever form of leadership we are called to, let us exercise it with one thing in mind. People don't fail because they want to fail. People fail because they don't know how to succeed.

CHAPTER TWENTY-ONE

RETURN TO VIRTUE

Eight hundred years ago, a young Italian man searching for meaning in his life went into a dilapidated old church and heard the voice of God speak to him, saying, "Rebuild my Church. As you can see, it is in ruins." If you and I listen carefully, I believe we will hear the same voice saying the same thing in our hearts today.

Francis' first response was to repair and rebuild a number of churches in and around Assisi, but the voice kept calling to him... "Francis, rebuild my Church. As you can see, it is in ruins."

Over the past twenty-five years, we have spent a lot of time, energy, money, and effort building and restoring the physical facilities of our churches. But the voice of God continues to call to us. Once again, God is saying, "Rebuild my Church." The rebuilding that needs to be done now is of a spiritual nature.

The Role of Virtue

The only way for our lives to genuinely improve is by acquiring virtue. It is impossible for a society to genuinely improve unless its members grow in virtue. The renewal that the Church is desperately in need of is a renewal in virtue.

The great fallacy of the lukewarm moral life is to believe that our sole responsibility is to eliminate vice from our lives. In the absence of a sincere and focused effort to grow in virtue, vice will creep into our lives unawares in the form of a hundred different self-destructive habits.

No man is born virtuous. Good habits are not infused. Virtue must be sought out and can only be acquired by continual practice. You learn to ride a bicycle by riding a bicycle. You learn to play baseball by playing baseball. You learn to be patient by practicing patience. You become virtuous by practicing virtue.

For thousands of years, politicians, philosophers, and priests have all argued about the best way to organize society. Many organizing concepts have been suggested: duty, obligation, law, force and obedience, to name but a few. If humanity is to flourish in the twenty-first century, it will be because we realize once and for all that the key-organizing concept of a truly great civilization is virtue.

The connection between virtue and the flourishing of an individual is unquestionable. To live a life of virtue is to move beyond the chaos and restlessness that agonize the human heart, and embrace a life of coherence. Similarly, the relationship between the virtue of the members of a community and the flourishing of the society in which they live is proven time and time again throughout history.

I have never met a thief or a liar who was truly happy or genuinely flourishing. If we ever hope to satisfy our desire for happiness, we must turn our attention toward the acquisition of virtue.

—*◦∿∿◦*—

On my eighteenth birthday, my mother and father gave me a card with Rudyard Kipling's poem "If" printed on the front. For years, I kept the card in the top drawer of my bedside table. Often, while I was laying awake at night pondering a situation in my life, I would read over these words. The poem contains a wonderful list of human virtues. Kipling's list is by no means complete, but it is filled with profoundly practical suggestions, and it certainly provides an inspiring starting point.

If you can keep your head when all about you
    Are losing theirs and blaming it on you,
If you can trust yourself when all men doubt you,
    But make allowance for their doubting too;
If you can wait and not be tired by waiting,
    Or being lied about, don't deal in lies,

Or being hated, don't give way to hating,
        And yet don't look too good, nor talk too wise:
If you can dream - and not make dreams your
        master;
If you can think - and not make thoughts your
        aim;
If you can meet with Triumph and Disaster
        And treat those two impostors just the same;
If you can bear to hear the truth you've spoken
        Twisted by knaves to make a trap for fools,
Or watch the things you gave your life to, broken,
        And stoop and build 'em up with worn-out
        tools:

If you can make one heap of all your winnings
        And risk it on one turn of pitch-and-toss,
And lose, and start again at your beginnings
        And never breathe a word about your loss;
If you can force your heart and nerve and sinew
        To serve your turn long after they are gone,
And so hold on when there is nothing in you
        Except the Will which says to them: 'Hold on!'

If you can talk with crowds and keep your virtue,
        Or walk with Kings - nor lose the common
        touch,
If neither foes nor loving friends can hurt you,
        If all men count with you, but none too much;
If you can fill the unforgiving minute
        With sixty seconds' worth of distance run,
Yours is the Earth and everything that's in it,
        And - which is more – you'll be a Man, my son!

—*ᴠᴠ*—

The Church has always proclaimed that the seven foundational virtues are the cornerstone of the moral life. This sevenfold foundation is made up of "the supernatural virtues" – Faith, Hope, and Love – and "the four cardinal virtues" – Prudence, Justice, Temperance, and Fortitude. The supernatural virtues free us from self-centeredness and protect us from the ultimate vice – pride. The cardinal virtues, which are sometimes referred to as "the human virtues," allow us to acquire the self-mastery necessary to make us free and capable of love.

The only way for our lives to genuinely improve is by acquiring virtue. To grow in virtue is to improve as a person. Virtues are the tools for building the-best-version-of-yourself.

The World Needs the Church

As I have already said, it seems the only acceptable prejudice in this hyper-sensitive, politically correct, modern climate, is to be anti-Catholic. This prejudice is growing and growing, as it is subtly nurtured by the arts and the media, and furthered by the way prevailing philosophies undermine Catholicism.

In the midst of the obviously anti-Catholic environment that our culture has created, it is easy to overlook some fundamental and practical realities. The world needs the Church today more than ever before. In a modern schema where people are becoming more self-absorbed and completely fixated on the fulfillment of their own selfish desires, the Church is only going to be needed more and more.

The Catholic Church feeds more people, clothes more people, houses more people, and educates more people than any other organization in the world. And when the modern media and the secular culture have finished tearing down the Church as best they can, let me ask you, who then will take our place? Who will feed the hungry? Who will clothe the naked? Who will visit the lonely and imprisoned? Who will house the homeless? Who will comfort the sick and dying? Who will educate the masses?

The world needs the Church. Even your hardened and cynical politicians with nothing in mind but personal gain recognize this reality with alarming clarity. If for no other reason than from an economic standpoint, they know they couldn't pick up the broken pieces that would be left if the Church disappeared from their community.

The Church may be massively unappreciated and woefully persecuted, but we must press on all the same. After all, that is always the way it has been. Jesus didn't promise an easy way. He promised that we would be ridiculed, persecuted, and unappreciated as he himself was, but that we would nonetheless experience joy and fullness of life.

We should try not to forget that when Jesus was on the cross, he didn't turn to the man next to him and say, "You did the crime, now pay the price." No, he offered him a better life. That is the responsibility that now falls to our shoulders as followers of Jesus. The mission of the Church is to offer people a better life.

The key word in all of this is "offer." The Church doesn't force people to do things. The Church is a lover who comes to propose to the beloved. The Church proposes to you a certain course of action for certain situations. The Church proposes to you and me a certain way of life. And each of us, like the beloved who is proposed to, must accept the proposal or turn down the proposal. But, whatever our decision, we must live with that decision forever.

About this Book

For a long time I have wanted to write this book, and yet, at the same time I wish I had another fifty years to prepare. In this book I have not sought to answer all the questions, nor have I tried to cover all the controversial issues. This book is not strictly speaking a theological work, nor is it a defense of Catholicism. It is not an attempt to change people's minds about the Catholic Church, and this is not a book that promises to deliver monumental virtue with seductive ease. I am also fully aware that it is not a book for everyone. It is merely my reflections on my experience as a Catholic and on Catholicism at this time. I have simply tried to share what I have witnessed, learned, discovered, and experienced about Catholicism thus far in my short life. In doing so, I have attempted to demonstrate that Catholicism is a program of life, a lifestyle, that encourages all who embrace it to become the-best-version-of-themselves.

The words on these pages are a celebration of Catholicism. A celebration of all it is and all it can be.

By reading them and applying them to our lives, I hope our lives become a celebration of Catholicism.

Something Wonderful is About to Happen

On my desk at the foundation I have a post-it note that simply says, "Something wonderful is about to happen!" It has been there for a long time now. I have thought of having these words printed in calligraphy and putting them in a nice frame... but there is something powerful about this simple post-it note.

I believe something wonderful is about to happen. I believe it in my life, I believe it in your life, and I believe it in the life of the Church. I pray you and I will make ourselves available to God so that he can use us to make it happen. You see, God doesn't always need or use the most talented people. Most of the time, he uses those who make themselves available. How available are you willing to make yourself to God?

It is true that the Church finds herself in the midst of a difficult time in her life. The present dilemmas that we face as a Church are a cause of sadness for all who love the Church. In mythology for thousands of years, it has been believed that the darkest hour is right before the dawn, and that in this hour of greatest darkness, the great heroes of the new times are being born. The darkness that the Church is passing through at the moment will not last. There is a light at the end of it all.

Sometimes people ask me what stops me from becoming depressed or falling into despair. Two things,

I tell them. In the first place, I know that the renewal that the Church so desperately needs is not my sole responsibility. And in the second place, hope. Where does the hope come from? What feeds that hope? It comes from God and neighbor. My hope comes from God who loves me and from my neighbor who loves me.

In a world filled with so much cynicism, the supernatural virtues – Faith, Hope, and Love – are often laughed at and dismissed as foolish and naive. Some people say that hope only sets you up for disappointment, and that it is a bad thing. Hope is a good thing, maybe the best of things. Hope is one of those things that you can't buy, but will be freely given to you if you ask. Hope is the one thing people cannot live without.

I hope...

I hope I can live up to the gifts and talents God has given me. I hope I can have the courage to be a true friend. I hope I never stop striving to become the-best-version-of-myself. I hope we can build a world where your children and my children can grow free and strong. And I hope we grow wise enough to realize that we have no better ally in achieving our hopes than Catholicism.

I hope...

Matthew Kelly was born in Sydney, Australia, on July 12, 1973. Over the past ten years two million people have attended his talks, seminars, and retreats. Against the backdrop of travel to fifty countries, millions more have been touched by his writings and appearances on radio and television programs.

Kelly's most recent books include *The Shepherd, The Rhythm of Life, A Call to Joy,* and *Mustard Seeds.* Collectively his seven titles have been published in seven languages and have sold more than 450,000 copies.

Both as a speaker and as a writer, Matthew Kelly possesses a powerful ability to combine the ageless tool of storytelling, with a profound understanding of today's culture and the highest Christian ideals. As a result he captures our imaginations and helps us to see our struggles in a new light. With his keen sense of humor and heart-warming charm, Kelly seems to effortlessly elevate and energize people to pursue the highest values of the human spirit.

Exploring the challenges of our modern world, Kelly brilliantly puts into context the unchanging truths of the life and teachings of Jesus Christ. From an age inordinately preoccupied with doing and having, Kelly's message rings our with a truth that is unmistakable challenging and attractive, "Who you become is infinitely more important than what you do, or what you have."

Matthew Kelly's message is both timely and timeless. His example is authentic and inspiring. His passion for life is refreshing and challenging. It is certain that he will continue to be, with increasing influence, one of the most sought-after and endearing Catholic voices of our time.

Whether you received *Rediscovering Catholicism* as a gift, borrowed it from a friend, or purchased it yourself, we're glad you read it. We think you will agree Matthew Kelly is a most refreshing voice in the Church today, and we hope you will share this book and his thoughts with your family and friends.

If you would like to order additional copies of this book, are interested in writing to the author, wish to receive his free newsletter – *The Beacon,* would like information about his speaking engagements, or would like to invite him to speak at your Church or to your group, please address all correspondence to:

The Matthew Kelly Foundation
2330 Kemper Lane
Cincinnati, Ohio 45206
United States of America

Phone: 1-513-221-7700
Fax: 1-513-221-7710
e-mail: info@matthewkelly.org
www.matthewkelly.org